W9-AHO-130

# Teardown

## *A Love Story*

Becky Burckmyer

Copyright 2020
All rights reserved
ISBN 978-0-578-81543-5

Cover design by Jill Breitbarth
Interior design by Alida Castillo


Charlotte Cecil Raymond
Literary Agent
32 Bradlee Road
Marblehead, MA 01945
(781) 631-6722
raymondliterary@gmail.com

This is a true story, though many names have
been changed to protect people's privacy.

*For Larry, who loved the house*

# PART ONE

# CHAPTER 1

My husband Larry died after a ten-year slide into dementia that left little of him recognizable. A brilliant, strong, creative man who had founded and run his own successful manufacturing firm and raised four children who were powerfully devoted to him, he was reduced to sitting in a corner of the room, arms crossed around his increasingly thin body as if to ward off who-knew-what scary fantasies or hallucinations.

"What's wrong, Larry? Are you worrying about something?" I'd ask.

"No, no, I'm all right. I'm glad you're home."

He'd seemed unsinkable—sturdily, even powerfully built, with electric blue eyes, a hearty pink complexion, and a shock of pure white hair—and he'd hurled himself at the world and everything in it with incredible assurance. Now he was so thin and diminished it was like having just half of Larry.

I couldn't get him to talk much. When he did talk, it was often in clichés, and with mind-numbing repetition of observations and criticisms set off by things he heard or saw. As I drove him around Marblehead, the little seacoast town just north of Boston that was our home, my mind began to feel deadened, my responses curtailed. On the subject of most Massachusetts politicians: "Left-wing liberal flakes." On trees: "Nothing but giant weeds." Environmentalists: "A bunch of tree-huggers." After I'd heard these a hundred times or so, I felt like crying. Or, as much as I loved him, smacking him in the head.

Not that I hadn't been warned. Gina, a couples therapist we'd visited a few years back, deciding Larry was distinctly ill in some way, sent him for testing to a colleague she knew. This woman told me

"Your husband has either Alzheimer's or Pick's disease."

"What is Pick's disease?

"Like Alzheimer's except you lose language. You can only cry out or yell. Your husband will die in a wheelchair, howling like a wolf, and death will be your friend."

Direct quote. Well, thank you. I didn't pay attention, because I had a brother in Virginia who was dying of cancer, and a mother who was chronically ill and broken-hearted over my brother's imminent death. I forgot about the testing as soon as possible. You can do this if you're highly motivated.

I never saw that woman again. But Gina became my therapist and has gotten me over some awful humps (such as the deaths of my brother and mother). I see her once a month now, because You Never Know.

After Larry retired and before I realized how ill he was—having a near-genius IQ, according to another psychologist, he was able to disguise his condition and mistakes—he'd made a number of risky investments, convinced they'd romp home and make us seriously rich. They didn't; 99 percent of them still haven't. He had also neglected to file our 2007 tax return, dropping it on his worktable in the basement and causing the IRS in a fury to delve into our IRAs and take what they felt they were owed, plus a considerable amount in fees. No doubt I could have thrown myself on their mercy, but I haven't heard anybody yet talking about how merciful the IRS is.

Occasionally Larry would rouse himself for a big-time argument. He'd always enjoyed that in his prime: he was unafraid of anyone else's opinions and even seemed to get a kick out of being a contrarian. That "trees are giant weeds" thing was obviously asking for a battle. During this time, we had an enormous fight over whether Muslim was a religious or an ethnic designation. He insisted that Muslims were all Arabs; I mentioned Croatia, Indonesia, and the Philippines in vain. We even had an argument over that thing about the tree falling in the forest and making no noise because no one was there to hear it. I can't even remember which side I took.

I'm still ashamed of myself for getting worked up over these.

And then one night he got up from our table—we'd had friends in for dinner—and announced it was time to go home. Our guests waited in horror to see whether I'd laugh or cry. I laughed, but it was almost the ultimate clue to how far he'd gotten from himself: Larry adored his house and was rightly proud of the work he'd done on it over the years and the wonderful collection of stuff he'd filled it with.

It was not long after that that he got hold of my car keys (the Registry of Motor Vehicles had taken his car away a full three years earlier) about 6:00 one morning and took off for parts unknown with no phone, no wallet, no credit cards. I got a call about four frantic hours later that the car battery had (mercifully) died and Larry and car were safe at an auto dealer's waiting for me. I almost wept with relief: what if he'd hurt himself, or someone else? I got him and the car home eventually, but then the phone calls started.

My daughter Sarah, four miles away in Swampscott, was besieged by concerned callers asking: "When is your mother going to do something about your father?"

We listened, realizing that in fact I'd been living in a fool's paradise, and I accepted that I couldn't really keep him safe. A wonderful retirement home nearby with a third floor for people with cognitive disorders had room for him. So our son Charlie borrowed a truck, and the kids and I moved Larry in. He was cooperative about staying in Bertram House, and seemed even to enjoy some of the entertainment, especially when the Activities leader led the Alzheimer's group in patriotic songs. He ate well at first, then lost interest in food and even in his evening martini. I took him home one day to watch a set of boats with different-colored sails match race—I'd thought he would love to photograph them. He had almost 200 cameras and lenses and a real passion for photography. At Christmas he might have four cameras going almost simultaneously. I put a camera with a zoom lens on the table where we sat for lunch, but he showed no interest at all. He didn't eat much. I asked whether he'd like to take a nap or go back to Bertram House. He opted for Bertram House. He lasted about two months and then, completely depleted but peaceful, died.

We had better luck than a lot of people: we were married for thirty-seven years, had two wonderful children together and many close, happy times, and when he died it was, despite an element of relief (of which I was not proud), a huge loss. Larry had been my rock, my booster—an enormous source of strength from the day we met. He told me I could do anything, and the power of his personality was such that I believed him. Fifteen years older than I, he seemed to understand how the world worked, and how to navigate through it.

"Larry, the bank wants me to put together a course on business writing and teach it to their senior management! What on earth am I going to do?"

"Make it up and teach it: you know how to do business writing. And charge them like heck for it! Banks have deep pockets and a big budget for professional development: they *need* to spend it. Why shouldn't they spend a hunk of it on you? And don't forget: you know more than anyone else in the class."

Talk about the wind beneath my wings.

How on earth did he know corporations had professional development budgets? I felt lost without him.

I'd gone through all the activities built around a death, amazed at just how incredibly busy one could be—notifying friends and relatives; fending off the scary men at the funeral home trying to sell me ornate urns and satin-lined caskets; distributing certificates proving Larry was who I said he was, certificates proving he was really dead, obituaries for local, city, school, and college newspapers (all slightly different); absorbing the word from McLean Hospital that Larry's dementia was indeed Alzheimer's; effecting name changes on IRAs; planning clothes for the funeral, making sure our son Charlie didn't try to wear white socks with his suit. Scattering Larry's ashes in the church's Remembrance Garden, on the water he'd sailed, and on the beach he'd loved. I'd given away most of Larry's clothes, which it pained me to look at, saving the beautiful sweaters for Charlie, who didn't want them. I'd tidied the paperwork he'd strewn haphazardly all over the china closet, literally knee-deep in places. And so on.

Then for a little while, I just sat. And then I sat some more.

It was very hard on the children, Charlie especially. Sarah was married with two toddlers. But Charlie wasn't really settled; and he was crazy about his father. He had a recurrent dream in which Larry appeared, alive and well.

"Dad! I thought you were dead!" he'd say in amazement.

Larry would put his finger to his lips with a puckish smile and tell Charlie, "Shhh! No one's supposed to know." This dream broke my heart, not to mention Charlie's.

Eventually I pulled myself together. Based on those unwise financial decisions Larry had made before I realized how ill he was, I was not in great shape financially. Justin, Larry's financial officer—now mine, I supposed—called. I'd been drawing out the sums I needed to live on from our joint accounts and, according to Justin, was dipping into principal.

Moderately ignorant about financial matters, even I knew this was a bad thing. I promised not to do it again if I could help it. But how *could* I help it? No money was coming in. My profitable career as a freelance writer and copy editor had foundered on the shoals of a bad car accident Larry had had, the demise of the publishing houses, and the Internet, which says you can write it any darn way that feels good to you. Who needed books, or, for that matter, correct English? I was a living anachronism. A new career at 65 seemed unlikely, at least not one that would pay our property tax, in five figures. I figured I could sell trinkets to tourists in one of Marblehead's many local boutiques, which would be fun, but that wasn't about to cover my needs. I had no income except from those investments Justin felt I was threatening. Clearly time for a change.

As I thought about my dilemma, I spun my desk chair around and looked out the window at the harbor filled with boats. What a view: so lovely that every morning as I brushed my teeth in the bathroom, I had to remind myself I wasn't on vacation. The rambling Victorian cottage, now well over 100 years old, was a monster to heat in the winter but a joy to live in most of the time. Almost all its rooms offered views of the harbor. Across the lane that ran in front of the house, a little staircase leading to a rocky beach beckoned.

Was it selfish to want to live alone in a house of this size? Shouldn't I let somebody else enjoy it? Someone with young kids? An architect who lives a couple of blocks from me, said, "Where is it written that the number of people in a house should correspond to the size of the house? You can live in a house as big or as small as you like, Becky: it's nobody else's business." That was kind of her, and very comforting.

So how to finance a life if I stayed here? I'd tried a couple of potential solutions while Larry was in the retirement home. Larry had collected a number of very nice marine paintings over the years, so I looked into selling some of those; he had talked with dealers who believed they might fetch a good deal of money. The reality seemed otherwise: I sold two paintings at auction, both for a fraction of their assessed value. I'd investigated selling the family silver on eBay, but nobody seems to want silver these days. That went double for the vases, sculptures, pitchers, perfume bottles, and our fantastic animal-shaped candlesticks: Larry never met an object he didn't want to collect. I also sold some gold coins, long-ago Christmas presents from Larry's parents, but housekeeping quickly swallowed the profits, and the price of gold spiked soon after, making me feel like a loser. Discouraged and tired with a fatigue that was more sadness and worry than anything else, I stopped trying to sell stuff.

A suggestion to our great friend and family lawyer Dudley that I might take out a reverse mortgage on the house had elicited such a reaction that I feared for his health, not to mention my own.

"Are you completely out of your [expletive deleted] mind? Sometimes I think you belong in a home. For a smart woman you can act like the stupidest knife in the drawer! A reverse mortgage is a piece of [expletive deleted]!"

Not a good plan, apparently: bad terms; hidden costs; duplicitous maneuvers that might force me out of the house and onto the street, apparently before I was dead. Whatever. That's how you learn, I mused.

That left one obvious option: selling the house. I knew it was a valuable piece of property, the house well built, and the third of an acre of land by the harbor a very attractive proposition. I called a real estate agent and looked at a few condos. Not the end of the world: after all, I'd had almost forty years to enjoy the house. My children had spent hours on the rocky beach, looking for treasures, swimming, and sailing any kind of craft they could get their hands on (including a much-prized chunk of Styrofoam). Maybe it was time to let another fortunate family raise their children here.

"I have bad news for you, sweetie," said my good friend Betsy. She and Phil, who ran a small real estate agency, had come by to have a drink on the porch and watch the sun set. "No young family is going to buy this house. They couldn't afford it. I know you love it—we all love it, and we've loved sharing it with you, but frankly, the place is a teardown."

I shot out of my chair. My gin and tonic rocked dangerously. "A teardown? A teardown?? What are you talking about? Why would anybody want to tear down this house?"

"Simmer down, Becky, hon," Phil said soothingly. "We're not bad-mouthing the house. It's a good place—"

"Good? What do you mean by 'a good place'? It's a fabulous place. Look how well it's built. Look at the heavy construction! Look at the wrap-around porch! Look at the detail in the moldings: it was built like a year-round house. Actually, it's built like a--"

"Becky, let me finish. You've lived here so long that you don't see the problems the house has: you're used to them and you work around them. Just as a f'rinstance, not everybody likes to cross a hall and run down half a flight of stairs just to brush their teeth. And the overhead

lights aren't exactly state of the art. Is it even safe to turn them on?"
He had me there. The bathrooms had been added some years after the
house was built—servants came cheap, and apparently the original owners
were happy with the chamber pot system—and were cantilevered out from
the second- and third-floor staircase landings. As for the lights, I'd never
really thought about them. They had push-button switches that my friends
either laughed at or waxed nostalgic over. Indirect lighting was the thing
nowadays, wasn't it? The overheads and Victorian lamps were indeed outdated. But that was surely no excuse to rip down 12 rooms' worth of house.

"Here's the thing," Phil continued. "You're sitting on a piece of land
that's worth three times what the house is worth. Anyone who can afford
to buy the whole package can afford to rip the house down and build one
with new plumbing, bathrooms adjoining every room, modern lighting,
and new, safe wiring." Phil laid his hand on my shoulder. "I realize this is
going to be hard for you to accept. But the good news is, with this view,
the property should command a small fortune. Do some minor cosmetic
work, sell when you're ready, and you'll walk away set for life."

"Hard to accept? You bet it's hard to accept. And I'm not accepting it,
because it's completely unacceptable. I'll sell everything in the house and
let it fall down around my ears before I'll let some idiot with more money
than sense flatten this house for no good reason."

Betsy and Phil exchanged a look and quickly turned the talk to their
daughter Megan's new job, and no more was said about teardowns. But I
went to bed angry and sorrowful. The very thought of the house facing
the wrecking ball filled my heart with grief. The news had been a sickening
jolt; and the worst part was that I could see Betsy and Phil were probably
right: if I sold, particularly to the wrong person, the house was very likely
to be torn down. I would have to find the right buyer. But how to find that
person? I shed some tears. I really loved the house so much, with its beautiful sunsets and warm breezes. And my whole family loved it: it was a kind
of touchstone for them, a place where they could go to remember who they
were. And to remember Larry. I couldn't lose it—I just could not.

# CHAPTER 2

I woke the next morning with the feeling that something bad was pressing down on my chest. In an instant I remembered the grim news: if I tried to leave the house, it was probably a teardown. The very existence of this beloved home depended upon me. If I sold it, it was likely to be razed to the ground. And there was no way I was going to let that happen. Just to sit on my upstairs deck in the spring sunshine; to take a swim off the little beach; to sit with a glass of wine on the downstairs porch; to cuddle under my quilts on winter nights and listen to the wind howl—all these were such a joyous part of my life that just to imagine being without them seemed an awful deprivation. As for watching it being sold and torn down: tears sprang unbidden to my eyes, and I felt an ache in my chest. This was love, pure and simple. And why shouldn't one love a house—even passionately?

My jaw firmly set, I began to take stock. What could I do? Prowling around the house, thinking hard, I remembered what Larry had told me about buying and improving it in 1965. When he and his first wife Molly discovered she was having twins, they realized they would soon outgrow their Beacon Hill apartment. It was time for a house. One Saturday afternoon when they had finished sailboat racing in Marblehead and were driving to the Corinthian Yacht Club for a party, they noticed a For Sale sign on a large white Victorian about two doors down from the club. Larry jotted down the number of the realtor, Barbara, and called her early the next week. "Oh, yes," she said. "That's Dave Bailey's place. It's offered at $30,000."

After Larry had thanked her and hung up, he and Molly agreed it was a lot of money, but they had to buy something: the babies were due in October, and it was already June. When Barbara showed them the house the following weekend, Larry told her they were definitely interested, but the price seemed high. "Offer him $26,000," she said. "His second wife doesn't like Marblehead, and he's eager to sell." Barbara was right.

You have to laugh, looking at housing prices nowadays. A Queen Anne/Stick Style Victorian built in 1881, with three floors, five bedrooms, and water views, for $26,000!

The house was built as a summer home by a retired carriage maker in Brookline, Massachusetts. As such, it featured few closets or other storage spaces, but Larry and Molly considered it a treasure. The decorative shingles, high ceilings, detailed moldings, and above all, wonderful views across Marblehead Harbor instantly charmed the couple. Its few bathrooms—far from the bedrooms, bizarrely located off the staircase landings, clad top to bottom in appalling gray plastic tile (the proud work of Mr. Bailey himself, a dedicated DIY specialist)—did not. But Larry was tactful enough to admire Mr. Bailey's remodeling and carpentry, and they got on well. The deal went through. The Baileys joyfully vacated to Boston, while the Burckmyers moved into 15 Corinthian Lane. Fortunately, they were settled in completely by the time the babies came, a bit early, as twins often do. Pandemonium ensued, but they made it through in good shape, with the beautiful little girls, Elizabeth, called Liza, and Mary, sleeping through the night at five months.

When they decided to redo the kitchen (which was in poor shape, needing new cabinetry and major appliances), it was hard on the couple, especially Molly, who had the pleasure of learning to do dishes in the bathtub upstairs. Worse: it was in fact very stressful. I found a letter Molly had written Larry on sheet after sheet of yellow legal pad paper:

> . . . I don't think you understand how hard this is for me. I'm trying to take care of the girls, and cook, and do dishes, and it's really difficult. I'm so tired. And I'm still trying to look nice when you come home. And I got my hair cut a week ago and you still haven't noticed. I feel very far from you somehow . . .

And so on in that vein. I almost wept. Poor lady.

Three years after they had moved in Molly moved out, taking the girls with her "back home" to Santa Fe. Larry was heartbroken: his girls were his world. He had also just started his new company, a sheet metal fabricating firm, in Peabody. Money was so tight he more or less stopped heating the house. I picture him walking around in a parka, blowing on his hands. That was around the time I met him. We were married in 1973.

As for me, I fell for the house the moment I laid eyes on it. I had a complete sense of homecoming because, for one thing, the first-floor plan is almost identical to that of the house I grew up in in Virginia. For another, it is built in a strong, almost masculine style, with big chunks of woodwork that seem to wrap their arms around you. The effect was heightened by the big, solid Empire furniture Larry had picked up here and there. I was blown away by the strong feeling of love I felt the instant I walked through the door. A flight of stairs leads up to the first floor, which has a wraparound porch on three sides. The front door opens into a broad hall with double doorways into the living room on your left, now pale pink with a lot of dark furniture and coral accents; and dining room, mostly mauve, and a small half-bath beyond on your right. Actually, it's possible to look clear through the living room: there's a very large picture window on the left wall that takes in the entire harbor. Amazingly, this was original with the house, though the Victorians weren't noted for their appreciation of light and air. If you look straight, the staircase to the second floor is to the left; to the right of the staircase, the hall continues back into the kitchen, which runs the width of the house.

Halfway up the stairs, a landing gives onto the first bathroom, and the same arrangement is encountered on the way up to the third floor—obviously these bathrooms were an afterthought, built some time after the house. There are three bedrooms and a study on the second floor, two bedrooms and a sort of junk room on the third. An attic with a pull-down set of stairs in the third-floor hall has terrified children for more than a half-century to my certain knowledge, and probably longer.

As I walked upstairs, I thought how much we'd improved all three bathrooms and the master bedroom. When we were first married, Larry and I had pulled off all the gray tile with crowbars. The downstairs bath featured a pattern of vines and climbing roses, and the floor was patterned in small hexagonal pink tiles. Larry had bought some dynamite antique metal dolphin-shaped fixtures: dolphins holding towel bars, biting toilet paper rolls, spitting into the green marble sink. I'd found a beautiful square turn-of-the-century stained-glass window in subtle pinks and greens.

We'd tiled the second- and third-floor baths in various blues and yellows, one with beautiful Italian marble floor tile.

Mr. Bailey had created two closets in the master bedroom on the second floor as well, which looked like large storage crates, of which he was also proud. They weren't attractive, but the idea was excellent, because as I mentioned, the retired gentleman who had had the house built had requested little in the way of closets. We hired a contractor to put in two closets flush to the bedroom wall with louvered doors. While he was at it, Larry suggested we bash holes in our bedroom wall and the room next to it and install big sliding doors onto a soon-to-be-erected deck. The contractor obliged, and the effect was fabulous.

Portion of a letter to friend Connie:

*Have just taken possession of my closet. When I opened the cabinet overhead, a very large pile of Molly's maternity underwear fell out on my head. I don't know whether to laugh or cry. Larry needs to be more careful. Much more careful*

I remembered how hard our first winter was, even though by now we were at least heating the house. I'd watched the curtains literally blowing in the living room beside the picture window: when the wind came out of the southwest, you really couldn't stay in the room. You couldn't even light a fire: the air would just blow down the chimney and you'd smoke up the whole first floor. An improvised damper at least kept the room a little warmer. The dining room (where the thermostat was) was the warmest real room in the house; the half-bath between the dining room and the kitchen stayed really, *really* warm. My parents, of course, wanted to visit. I remembered sitting in the half-bath writing them, "Why not wait till it's nice weather outside? We can take walks, maybe go out on the boat, have lunch at the café outdoors." In fact, I was a little concerned that the two elderly Southerners might not survive when the southwest wind started blowing in earnest.

The second year, when Sarah was born in May, Larry's business had turned the corner and we began making more considerable home improvements. Foam was blown in to keep the house, especially the exposed southwest side, warmer. We put thermopane in the picture window, and the living room curtains ceased to wave in the wind. And we tore out the front yard and put in a garage and a driveway, flanked by a beautiful array of trees and plants. When Charlie made his appearance two and a half years later, Larry celebrated, with help from Bam, a talented carpenter with an anthropology degree from Yale, by cantilevering the harbor end of the kitchen out about five feet, throwing an I-beam in under it, and making a real room out of what had been essentially a hallway with a drafting desk in it. He added some beautiful old lead-paned windows of varying shapes and sizes. These not only looked nice, but let in light while minimizing our view of the house directly next door.

Larry, who had collected furniture and paintings since he was a very young midshipman stationed in the Boston Naval Shipyard, was delighted to have room for the tables, chairs, and lamps and the wall space for many nautical and several Victorian genre paintings. He had a really good eye. We put in a comfortable sofa, a television, and a lot of toys. Instant family room! We spent a great deal of time there. Larry installed a big flagpole on the harbor side, and we were done.

I'd found the remodeling hard to take—I'm not crazy about change, and I thought the house was fine as it was, albeit cold. To make matters worse, Sarah was a fretful, tearful baby. When the rock ledge in the front yard was being dynamited to put the driveway in, I thought both of us would go crazy. Charlie was a sleepy, easy baby who didn't really notice the family room remodeling, and Sarah by that time was incredibly cheerful. In any case, the results were worth it: the house looked terrific and was super-livable. The yard was small, but there was a little garden out back and a tiny side yard. And most amazingly, right across the road, a set of steps led down to the rocky little beach. What a fantastic place to swim, especially if you like cold water! Or to teach a child to swim, or read a book in the sun, or just sit and look out across the harbor. When Larry's twins visited, they loved to look for hermit crabs, snails, and little green crabs in the tide pools to the right of the steps. We built drip castles, decorated them with shells and beach glass, and ringed them with moats. In the winter, Larry and I watched as the snow blew across the harbor and the few boats left in the water bucked and pitched at their moorings.

Teardown? No way! How could anyone even consider tearing this house down? I felt the tears start and impatiently brushed them away. I needed to generate ideas, not tears.

I decided to get out of the house and go for a drive. As I drove through Old Town, I was still thinking about the house. Betsy and Phil were probably right. Whoever bought my house might rip it down and start over, probably with something modern and glitzy. The thought made me almost sick. If I could get it fixed up—maybe there was a plumber who could fit some bathrooms into my bedrooms—then might I find a buyer who'd keep the house instead of tearing it down? I'd had little experience with being a contractor or even using one, and I didn't exactly have a lot of money to spend on such a project. A good idea, but I could lose my shirt and have little to show for it. My wonderful house—the house that everyone loved to come to--! Didn't I owe it to my kids, my stepkids, and the memory of Larry to try to save it? At this point I began to cry so hard I had to pull over. It took me awhile to pull myself together and continue my drive.

I was sitting at a traffic light in the middle of town when it suddenly came to me. I almost jumped out of the car in my excitement. I wanted to share the house with people who would appreciate it; I needed money; I loved to entertain. It was so obvious. I would open a bed and breakfast!

The more I thought about it the more excited I became. I knew several people who had been doing this for ages. They seemed to be managing the lifestyle and even enjoying it! I could use all the pretty linens, good china, and silver that the kids didn't want. I had three good extra bedrooms and two baths. Pillows, bedspreads, towels, bathmats—most of it was already in place. The guests would have the view, the porches, the beach. Old Town Marblehead was five minutes away, with its shops and restaurants. Why shouldn't I? How hard could it be? I called my son Charlie and asked him to meet me at the house.

# CHAPTER 3

"No, Mumz, you cannot open a bed and breakfast in this house," my son Charlie said wearily.

"Why ever not?"

"Well, it's a great house, but…"

"But what? What is wrong with it?"

"Please don't get your feelings hurt, but in the first place, it's a train wreck."

"What on earth is that supposed to mean?" Another person bad-mouthing the house: what else was new? Charlie, much like his father, was usually so supportive of anything I wanted to try. I was really hurt by his lack of enthusiasm.

"Mom, there's a string holding the gutter pipe onto that end of the porch." He pointed at the offending rig. "Not even a rope: a piece of *string*! And there's a wrecked bicycle that's been lying in the corner of the yard for three years. You can leave it there as long as you want, but you can't expect guests to pay to look at it."

"Are you kidding me? That stuff is all easy to fix. I could go out there and get rid of the bike in five minutes. Anything else?"

"Mumzi, you know what I mean. It's not your fault, but the house is really not in good shape. Regular maintenance hasn't been done on it since Dad got sick."

He was right, I realized. Larry had been handy: we'd never needed to call a carpenter, plumber, or electrician. He'd even wired most of the house himself. And for the last couple of years I'd been so occupied with his illness I hadn't given a thought to things like rotting boards on the porch or paint on the shutters and elsewhere. It hadn't seemed important. Now I took a hard look. The house, once gleaming white, was dingy with accumulated dirt, and the paint had begun to peel. There were missing shingles on the roof of the house and porch, and boards needed replacing, it seemed, everywhere.

"I see what you mean: the outside could use some work."

"And that's just the outside, Mumz. I really hate to say this, but inside is worse!"

"Oh, come on. What's wrong with it?" I was putting on a brave face, but inside I was crushed. I knew Charlie loved the house, really loved it. And I couldn't believe he honestly meant what he was saying. The house a mess, inside as well as out? It felt physical, so personal, almost as if my heart were hurting.

"The hall rug is in really bad shape all the way up the stairs. The paint in the living room is peeling. Have you not noticed the huge stain on the dining-room ceiling?

"The third-floor bathroom tub takes five minutes to drain: when you shower, the water's up over your ankles. Both bedrooms on the third floor are shabby: they need paint, curtains, and if possible a total makeover. Shall I go on?"

I thought about it. "Maybe we should make a list. I bet I can do a lot to fix it up myself."

"You're going to need help. I can do a little, but I don't have a lot of time. You'll need a handyman and probably a painter, too."

Daughter Sarah's concerns were different. "Mom, have you actually talked to people who've run bed and breakfasts? Have you read books or articles? I've heard everyone thinks they can run one, but it turns out it's an unbelievable amount of work. You're going to have to hire help, and that costs money! After you pay them, how much is that going to leave you with? You won't have a lot left."

This was discouraging, of course, and probably true. But what if I fixed these house issues and did all the housework and serving myself? Anybody could make a bed; fixing breakfast was a snap—I'd been doing it for years. Laundry, too. I decided to move ahead with my plans.

Of course Charlie eventually cooperated. He had recently graduated from business school, and he did some complicated work with spread-sheets to show me what I'd need to spend on breakfasts and sundries and the number of beds I'd have to fill for X number of nights to clear enough money to make the enterprise worth my while. I paid attention to the bottom line: I had my work cut out for me for sure. And it made sense to cut costs everywhere I could.

On the other hand, I wanted to make it nice for my guests, and that was going to take some money. I was determined that they weren't going to get el cheapo jam on their English muffins if I could help it.

"Mom, the most important thing is just getting the people to come," Charlie said. "I know you can do the rest. We need to create a really nice website for you, to drive the customers to your door. I know a guy who does websites: we'll get it set up with pictures and key words and . . ."

I stopped listening. A website? That *would* cost money!

I didn't know the half of it. I needed a license: that wasn't too bad. A bored town employee asked me the name of my B & B. I told her Harbor Gables. She wrote up what she called a business certificate and charged me $40. That was OK. But my friend Donna, owner of the Flying Cloud B & B, was adamant. "No! That isn't any good. Your name needs to say what you offer that's unique, and that's your harbor view. Call it Marblehead on Harbor! The town's name will ensure that you come up when people Google, and 'Harbor' tells them you're smack on the water."

She was right, of course. A brilliant idea. What a valuable friend! Back I went to the Town Clerk's office; another $40 and I was in business as Marblehead on Harbor (MoH). Next I had a visit from the Fire Inspector that ended with me in full panic mode, having been required to purchase ten smoke alarms and two sirens hardwired to ADT, plus two carbon monoxide detectors. Don't even ask how much this cost. Then I called my insurance agent and got another ugly surprise: my homeowner's insurance would drop me the minute they knew I was running a B & B! Insurance companies don't like B & Bs because they are sure the guests are damaging your furniture, stealing your stuff, and falling down the steps and suing.

"Maybe this enterprise could be our little secret," I suggested to Dave.

"No, Becky," he replied. "In fact, I'll be calling them as soon as we hang up to tell them: it's a requirement." That hurt my feelings and was also disconcerting. I needed more coverage if I was to run a business in my house, not less.

Luckily, my friend Susan, who has run a B & B for years, kindly gave me her insurance company's name. Disaster turned to triumph as I wound up with *more* coverage, including so-called trip-and-fall insurance, for the same money as before. She and Ruth, another veteran B & B owner, also set me straight on where the B & B business comes from. I'd distributed about a hundred folded brochures printed in color at Staples around the town, having a naïve idea that people would pick one up at the library, the yacht club, the drug store, or the Chamber of Commerce's cute little booth in the middle of Old Town, staffed on a volunteer basis by two adorable women who pass out literature on Marblehead's history and amenities. The leaflet is an outdated concept, as you probably realize. I don't think I ever met even one guest who'd seen one and chosen my B & B as a result. A completely wasted effort.

"Of course, the Internet is where the business comes from nowadays, for the most part. And you know about Availability Online, don't you?" asked Susan. "It's that terrific feature on the Chamber of Commerce website that lets people know at a glance whether you have a room or rooms available. Of course, you have to keep up to date with it, blanking out the rooms that are taken as soon as you book guests. The Chamber's information booth takes a look at this and recommends or calls you if you have rooms available. This can boost business a lot, along with word of mouth, of course."

And a wonderful thing happened out of the blue. I'd met a woman who ran a lovely B&B a block up the street from me, with *ten* bedrooms. One morning, she called me. "Becky, I've decided I'm not going to run the B & B this year—in fact, I probably never will again. My kids are three, five, and eight, and it's getting harder and harder to manage them with all their activities, and homework, and playdates. I was wondering whether I could refer my customer list to you. I actually have quite a big list—I've been running the B & B for seven years now—some guests have become good friends, and I feel very responsible for them. I would feel so much better if I could refer them to your place, which has the harbor views they all expect when they call." *Could she refer her customers to me?? What a windfall for MoH!* I had the florist send her a large basket of flowers on Mother's Day—but how can you thank someone who's done such an amazing thing for you?

Charlie worked on getting me a website, and his friend Wendy took appealing pictures of the bedrooms, public rooms, garden, and of course the harbor views, complete with the white Pawley's Island hammock slung across the corner of the porch. She also used some pictures from the Larry archives. I then got hooked up with a host for my website (ka-ching!) and joined the Marblehead Chamber of Commerce and Trip Advisor, which would respectively advertise my availability and charms (ka-ching!). Not to mention the lovely blue and gold wooden Marblehead on Harbor sign over the garage. Ka-ching all around.

I *know* you have to spend money to make money, but I was a wreck by the end of all this, turning out my empty pockets like the guy in the cartoon. And this didn't even include the services of the world's most creative, hardworking, mildly off-the-wall handyman, Ben, and his eccentric helpers, Darcy and Phil, who were tackling the exterior of the house as well as spackling, grouting, painting, fixing roof leaks, even replacing the old, drafty third-floor bathroom and bedroom windows. They also put a gorgeous new ceiling and shelves in the second-floor bathroom. Though terrified of the expense, I quickly grew besotted with the beautiful results. Darcy went through the rooms doing some sort of magic with a sponge to "brighten" the old paint, and Ben and Phil repainted the master bath walls and floor and the seaside third-floor bedroom. I made blue and white curtains for that room: swags and jabots (both new words to me), of which I was ridiculously proud. And Ben and Phil were hard at it on every sunny day replacing boards, pressure washing, and touching up paint. Then Susan and Ruth, who between them have more than 50 years of B & B experience, each came over and made suggestions that were enormously helpful. Ruth took one look at the blue third-floor hall carpeting. "Get rid of this. The plain wood underneath would look better, and if you have a pretty area rug, that would be better yet."

"What's wrong with the carpet?"

"Becky, you need new glasses. It has an enormous red stain in the middle of it." I'd lived with it so long I hadn't noticed. This was true of a lot of things—and the ladies pointed out every single one of them.

The kids and I gave the four bedrooms nautical names: a clever touch, we thought.

On the second floor, the beautiful bedroom with the king bed and sliding doors giving onto the deck and harbor view became Starboard Home. It had been our master bedroom. (I planned to move across the hall into Charlie's old bedroom, which had bunk beds and fabulous fish pictures all over the walls.) Starboard Home was painted in shades of sage, and I had painted each of the paneled closet doors in a pattern of olive, turquoise, and cherry red to match the bedspread. Also on the second floor was Amidships, the twin bedroom, which got beautiful morning sun and featured spanking white bedspreads and blue and cream draperies, which were sold by my dear friend Martha to me "at cost" (read "almost free"). The third-floor aerie with beach and harbor view, antique pastel flowered quilt, navy blue rug handed down when our friends' son left for college, and those remarkable homemade curtains was called Seaview. The fourth bedroom was a problem. It was a repository for furniture, rugs, lamps, and paintings that weren't quite good enough to put in the other rooms and didn't match each other. A double bed (barely) with a head and footboard and two ugly mismatched bookcases loaded with a hodgepodge of books completed the not-so-pretty picture. I thought it might be good for someone with small children—they could fit a Pack 'n' Play in there and use the bed as a changing table. Or two couples who liked each other could take both rooms and share the bath, as long as one couple were short, because of the footboard. I decided to name it Steerage, with a view to truth in advertising.

"How about Bilge?" suggested Sarah. That seemed a little harsh, even for an ugly room.

I found some baskets in the china closet and shopped at CVS and Walmart for travel-sized toiletries such as toothbrushes and toothpaste, shower caps, and shampoo and conditioner to put in each bathroom. Marshall's and Target yielded rich supplies of shower gel and hand lotion, and I got extravagant and bought two shower caddies. I also invested in 300 individually wrapped soaps I found online at a super-low price. They had an impossibly upscale name—Lord & Mayfair—and looked beautiful in the amazon.com picture. Amazingly, when they arrived they turned out to smell as good as they looked. And I put trays in each room to hold an assortment of goodies—sherry in a carafe, small Waterford crystal glasses, lots of bottled water, trail mix, wrapped chocolates, and so forth.

This was all heartening—I felt as if I was making progress, which made me less inclined to panic. Thanks to Susan, I even put in place a system to handle guest reservations. When she gets an email, phone call, or letter (rare), she takes out a brightly colored index card and writes the person's name, dates of arrival and departure, and room choice or choices (people often ask for more than one room). She includes address, email address, and phone number, and inquires about allergies and special preferences: Are they vegetarian? Allergic to nuts? Do they need to be on the first floor? She asks for a deposit of half the total for the rooms times the number of nights, and when she receives this, records the deposit and puts the guest-to-be on a large master calendar. If no deposit arrives, she calls to resolve the issue. On the day someone or several people are due to arrive, she tapes the card(s) to her kitchen counter where she can't miss them.

"And then I whisk through the rooms to make sure everything is ship-shape," Sue added. "I dust, and I add fresh flowers from the garden. I change the beds the minute a guest leaves: that way, if I get a guest or a family at the last minute, I'm ready."

This system has worked for her for more than twenty-five years. I bought cards and calendar and hoped it would work for me.

She also showed me a beautiful binder in which she puts restaurant and takeout menus from area eateries. It features a lot of her calligraphy on the cover and between sections.

"You do have to update the menus pretty often," she observed, "because the restaurants are always changing them. But it makes it so easy for the guests."

This looked like fun, so I grabbed menus from all over town, plus Salem, put them alphabetically into a binder, and wrote Menus on the front cover. It didn't look like Susan's, but it's a wonderful idea and a great help when advising guests.

Did I mention that Susan is a serious domestic goddess? The art and craft involved in creating a lovely home seem to come naturally to her. It helps that she is well organized and a hard worker. But beautiful flower arrangements from her garden and breads from her kitchen seem to appear out of thin air. Ruth, my other friend in a long-term relationship with her B & B, is the same: she gets up at 5:00 a.m. to bake bread. From scratch. Mine usually comes out of a box.

As you may have guessed by now, I am not a domestic goddess. One New Year's Eve I was having a large party and had had no time to take down the Christmas decorations throughout the house. There was a reason: this was the year that Charlie, just two years old, had eaten, in quick succession, a cigarette butt, a large chunk of leaves from the mountain laurel rope on the bannister, and an entire red glass Christmas ball. The poison control center and I became good friends, bonding over the best way to administer Ipecac. (Note: You do not make the person who has swallowed a Christmas ball throw up: you push Wonder Bread and hope for the best.) Charlie survived, and I threw spools of paper confetti at the tree and called it a New Year's tree. I don't think domestic goddesses have to do things like that. They keep better track of their children, for one thing, and they have much higher standards.

As improvements were made to the house, Sarah and Charlie appeared at intervals, offering suggestions and support as they were able, though both were busy with their jobs. Sarah brought jams and jellies for breakfasts and offered practical suggestions; she'd also, coincidentally, given me a Keurig one-cup coffee and tea brewer a few birthdays before, perfect for a B & B. Charlie kept a weather eye on Ben, who is a conspiracy theorist and occasionally would go off on tangents or on his motorcycle, making sure there was a new project on the runway as soon as the current one showed signs of completion. We couldn't afford to have him roar off and get busy with someone else's job.

"Why don't you aim to open just before Hallowe'en?" suggested Donna. "Everyone in the world comes to Salem for Hallowe'en, so you'll get some business. You can get your feet wet and decide whether you want to keep on with the B & B."

Another excellent idea. Where I would've been without my family and friends I cannot imagine.

Friends Joanne and Debbie came over one night for a few glasses of wine and offered more advice, including some Don'ts. They've visited a lot of B & Bs and they know what they don't like.

"Okay, Becky, no matter how much you're tempted, do not spend money on those awful shell things," said Joanne. "I actually think they're kind of creepy. And I know I'm not alone."

"You mean Sailor's Valentines?" said Debbie.

"Yes, those. Becky, you've seen them, yes? They're usually behind glass, which is a good thing, because Someone might be inclined to vandalize them. They're those great big, usually pale pink, hearts made out of shells."

"It's kind of sad," said Joanne. "It must've taken months to make one! Imagine how bored you'd have to be at sea to create something so labor intensive. And after all that work the end result is sort of ugly. But there are B & B owners who line their walls with them. I can't imagine what they're thinking."

"A lot of those sailors also did scrimshaw while waiting for the whales to show up," I said. "And some of these decorated tusks and bits of ivory are remarkable, beautiful, and very valuable." As you can imagine, Larry collected several of them and used to hide them in the wood box. He was afraid they'd be stolen. One foot-long tusk boasts a fabulous portrait of Admiral Nelson, a man I admire greatly—Larry, knowing this, bought it as a birthday present for me one summer. (Maybe it sounds odd, but I prefer it to many presents I've gotten. My friend Connie's double CD of Nelson-era British music, "England Expects," is a close second.)

"While we're at it, here's another thing I really dislike," Joanne said. "A lot of B & Bs have embroidered samplers or simply printed messages teaching you how you ought to live your life. When I'm on a trip, I don't want anyone telling me how to live. 'No Doubt the Universe Isn't Unfolding as It Should' is my motto."

"Another no-no," Debbie said. "Lots of B & Bs load up the bed with heaps of fat, fringy pillows. You need to resist the impulse. If your guests throw them on the floor they'll have to wade through them to reach the bed or the bathroom. It could make them trip."

"I agree totally," I said, "And as Dave Barry says, you are not allowed to *use* these pillows anyway: they're just decorations. It's not always easy to find the one you're supposed to sleep with."

"Also," said Joanne, "Do not under any circumstances hawk any so-called wonder products, like silver polish or marmalade or apple candy— the best in the world! In fact, the distance between the best apple candy in the world and the worst is not that great."

"I solemnly promise. A little more wine?"

"Thanks. And I'm sure you'd never make the guests throw a ball for your pet dachshund to catch," added Joanne. "In fact, maybe don't have the dachshund in the first place."

"Not a chance. If you catch me getting a dog *or* forcing it on the guests, you'll know I've lost it," I replied. "I've been the guest throwing that ball, and there's no question the dog will die of exhaustion before it will stop playing this game. Or the guest will."

I absorbed all this excellent advice and put it to use every chance I got. But as October drew near, I found it hard to keep calm: I worried that no one would come. If they came, they wouldn't like the house. If they liked the house, they'd hate the breakfasts. And so on. Then one late September afternoon, in a particularly neurotic state, I went into the second-floor bathroom and saw in absolute horror that the bathtub sported an orange stain about four feet long, and it looked exactly like a skeleton! The color was like rust, or iron, and literally, it had ribs and everything. I let out a shriek, and my wonderful twice-a-month house cleaner, Diana, came running.

"What on earth is this??" I screamed.

"Oh, my God, I have no idea!" she screamed back. "That is so scary! Where did it come from? The tub was fine when I finished."

You couldn't expect anybody to get into the shower with *that* in the tub. We tried everything: Ajax, Clorox, Fantastik, even salt, and vinegar.

Nothing had the slightest effect. The long bright-orange shape grew, if any-thing, more intense; the skeleton, whoever he was, seemed intent on stay-ing with us. I knew laying down new porcelain was expensive; to put an entire new plastic tub over mine would also cost a mint, and this tub was so old probably no plastic tub would fit anyhow. But I didn't have much choice: I had to do something. This was my "fancy" bathroom, which went with the room with the king-size bed and the private deck. I went to bed feeling even more broke and scared than usual.

I woke in the middle of the night—I'll never know where the inspira-tion came from—and said out loud, "Hydrogen peroxide!" I jumped out of bed and ran for the bottle, grabbed a cotton ball, saturated it, and threw it at the skeleton. In less than ten seconds, sure enough, he began to vanish. I stood there, awed, in the presence of a miracle.

I guess that for some reason the iron tub bled through the porcelain, thinned over many years. But why that bizarre shape? And why did it hap-pen then, and never again? Diana is convinced it has to do with bleach and won't use it in the tub: I have in fact used bleach when necessary and Skeletor hasn't reappeared. It's a mystery. But I can tell you for certain that it sapped what little was left of my confidence.

Around the first of October I had a call: a lady was looking for a room for two nights later in the month. My first guest! My mouth went dry and my heart started to hammer.

"You'd love Starboard Home," I stammered, leading with my ace. "It has a private deck and a king-size bed."

"I'm coming with my friend Doris," she answered drily. "I don't think we'll be needing a king-size bed." We agreed the twin bedroom would work.

You learn to ask the right questions first. Her name was Rita, and she was coming to Cambridge with Doris. I dutifully wrote up my index card and asked her to send a deposit, which she did; I checked on the card that she'd paid, and up went her name on the calendar. I was in business.

The thing that amazes me in retrospect is that Larry died at the be-ginning of June, and the B & B opened as planned four months later, on October 15. It's hard to believe we got so much done in such a short time, while dealing with the death industry as well. In addition to everything that workers, friends, and family did, I suspect I had a few angels helping me.

# CHAPTER 4

In addition to Rita and her friend Doris, I got a few more October bookings, which both delighted and frightened me. One was from a young woman from New Hampshire.

"My friend and I are witches," she told me.

"You're in luck," I said, "Marblehead on Harbor is witch friendly." The witches planned to stay two nights, October 30 and 31 and were excitedly anticipating their first visit to Salem.

Several couples who wanted to go leaf-peeping also called. A young lady and her new husband booked for October 30 and 31. (The mother of all costume parties takes place in neighboring Salem on the 30th.) And an older couple from the West Coast also booked in for those two nights: I was on my way: people believed in the B & B and were actually coming to stay!

I had not yet, however, had my first guests—Rita and her friend Doris from Yonkers. The thought of it kept me awake at night. Sarah laughed at me.

"What are you worrying about? There's nothing not to like, starting with you. You're not that awful, Mom. And look at the harbor! They're going to love it here."

I wasn't so sure. Rita and Doris sounded darned scary to me—Rita in particular: extremely sure of herself and maybe sort of picky. I could imagine her tasting the complimentary sherry in her room and spitting it across the room. I realized this was negative thinking, but I couldn't seem to turn it off. I tightened the sheets on the twin beds again and again, picturing Rita trying to balance a nickel on them and becoming very angry when she couldn't.

I'd decided on a buffet-style breakfast for MoH, and I rehearsed, setting out dishes and serving utensils on the family sideboard. I had some pretty bone china from my Virginian family with a laurel pattern in a wreath around the edge in pale blue, and white linen place mats with scalloped blue edges. White linen napkins embroidered with "McC" (abbreviation for my maiden name) completed the picture. I smiled as I laid out my mother's big silver spoon in her Kirk pattern, remembering how many times I'd seen it on that very sideboard at Thanksgiving dinner. I wondered what she'd think of this enterprise. Not much, probably: Mother was a traditional girl, and in her lexicon ladies did not work. This led to some dispirited thinking about my situation, so I plunged into vacuuming, which effectively shut it off.

You know how these things work—eventually October 16 finally did come around, the day of Rita and Doris's visit. I was wildly nervous all day. Even my 6:00 p.m. cocktail with Wolf Blitzer on CNN didn't calm me down. Rita had called again. Both ladies were working but planned on taking off early to try to avoid as much New York traffic as possible. She guessed they'd now arrive about 8:00. By that time, my teeth had literally begun to chatter.

8:30 came, then 9:00. Then 9:30, then 10:00. No Rita. Sarah called to make sure all was well. I told her no news and no guests. By this time I was such a wreck I was hoping they weren't coming and I'd get to keep the deposit. Maybe I could make that a way of life. Sarah said she was coming over: the kids were asleep and John was home.

She arrived with a bottle of Scotch. Good idea. We sat and drank Scotch and invented scenarios explaining Rita and Doris's absence. They were in a massive traffic jam. There'd been a death at someone's place of work. Rita's house had burned to the ground. Eleven o'clock came.

The doorbell rang. Showtime! In they came, loaded with suitcases, canvas bags, and apologies. They'd gotten lost and wandered around, not only in Connecticut, but apparently in the greater Boston area. I apologized for the Commonwealth's incredibly unfriendly policy of never putting a sign on any major road. You're just supposed to know where you are. I decided a good B & B hostess doesn't ask why someone would be five hours late and not call. Sarah chatted with us for a few minutes, then took off. I was alone with my guests.

Rita in person was very much like Rita on the phone: an imposing presence. About my age, she was a handsome woman with iron-gray hair, a prominent nose, and eyes that seemed to take in her surroundings at a glance. It was hard to tell what she thought of them. Doris was soft, gently graying, and slightly rounded, about the same age. While Doris admired the house and everything in it, Rita just stared. The two would have made a great good cop/bad cop team.

I got them settled in their room; we agreed on an 8:30 breakfast, and I collapsed into bed, more dead than alive.

Breakfast went off without a hitch: fresh fruit, juice, cereal, quiche, yogurt, and English muffins were on the menu and seemed to go down well. I learned that they were doing the Boston tourist thing and also visiting Rita's son, who lived and worked in Cambridge. I admitted under questioning that they were my first-ever guests. They assured me I was doing fine.

The next morning they had zucchini bread, hard-boiled eggs and bacon with the fruit, cereal, and yogurt, and took off. Rita said she visited her son quite often and would be calling me regularly. I was overjoyed. They signed the guest book saying they'd loved being at MoH, that it was like "visiting a dear friend," and vowed to be back very soon.

I never heard from them again. But they had given me a special gift, getting me over the first-time hurdle and making me feel good about it. I will always remember them—and of course I knew two strangers would never be that scary again.

Guests came. Predictably, they weren't as frightening as Rita. I was busy. I baked toll house cookies and put them in the front hall. I worried about my beloved state-of-the-art Maytag washer and dryer. If guests stayed just one night, I did many loads of laundry. I was also inclined to forget to bring, for example, more sherry to the third-floor bedroom. This sort of inefficiency meant many, many trips up and down stairs. I lost seven pounds without trying.

October flew by until it was time for the witches and warlocks.

The Halloween weekend arrived and with it Francie and Kay, the little witches from New Hampshire. To my surprise, they really were witches, to the extent they'd dressed the part: they arrived in green and purple tinsel wigs, pointy black hats, oceans of eye makeup, and striped stockings. In private life, they were both married with young children and good jobs in insurance and nursing. We sat up late talking. They said they liked hearing my stories—needless to say, this made me adore them. When Kay presented me with a check for her half of their stay, I was startled to see the name of a well-known nineteenth-century poet in the upper left-hand corner. An English major in college, I reacted with much excitement.

"Omigosh! Are you related?"

"That's my husband. He says he's named for some dumb old author in his family."

(Said dumb old author had penned the immortal line, "What is so rare as a day in June?")

Cindy and David showed up from California, also in fantastic Hallowe'en gear. She was tall and blond, the quintessential California girl, and her black witch costume was wildly becoming. Her boyfriend David told me her father was a well-known country western singer. David was rigged out in a Dickensian outfit complete with ruby red waistcoat, stove-pipe hat, and cape. He gave me advice that warmed my heart:

"Becky, why would you ever let this house go? Do whatever you have to do to keep it. You'd never be able to get another place like this."

The third Hallowe'en couple, Jennifer and Louis, looked about 36—if you added up their ages. They'd been married just a couple of months and were delighted to share stories and pictures of their wedding. I will look at anyone's wedding pictures, but these were adorable. They were too short of money to take anything but Steerage. But when we passed Seaview on the way to Steerage, I decided these honeymooners needed to take it. The look on their faces was utterly worth the loss of revenue.

The night of the costume party they came downstairs and stunned us all. He was a pirate, with everything except mustaches-on-fire, she a Pierrette, complete with little red lipstick circles on her cheeks and looped braids beside her ears. Cindy and David were handsome in their black, and the little witches, Francie and Kay, were charming in their tinsel and stripes.

I should mention that the witches were back the following Hallowe'en. Looking out the window at the frostbiting sailors, Kay asked me, "Do you mean they just sail around and around those markers? And then do it again?" They agreed that it sounded incredibly boring. I had never heard such a take on sailing: if Larry, an avid sailor, had been alive he would have found it the worst kind of heresy. Their unconscious iconoclasm made me laugh.

When that first October and Hallowe'en were over, Marblehead on

Harbor shut down pretty much until April of the next year. I was able to resist renting out rooms that Thanksgiving and Christmas, despite the seasonal longing for extra money. The disruption I create at those holidays is bad enough without having guests roaming the halls in need of wrapping paper. I was feeling simply wonderful: couldn't believe I'd done it; couldn't believe I'd made money; couldn't believe my bed and breakfast was a real going concern. Actually, it was a lot like hosting our friends over the years —except that I fixed just one meal a day for them, they provided their own entertainment (I often included a bottle of wine to add to the fun), and when they left they paid me! What a deal.

At Christmas, it's customary for the bed & breakfast owners in town to throw themselves a party. Chamber of Commerce folks and any significant others who may want to attend are also invited. A lot about how the business works can be learned just from talking to these (largely, but not entirely, female—married, divorced, or single) proprietors. It's also fun to get to see one another. Sometimes, when you have no room, you'll call one of the other B & B hostesses to see if they do and are feeling hospitable. However, you may not know them except by voice. This party helps close the gap.

Interestingly, there's usually more business chasing the B & Bs than the reverse. A good-sized wedding with a lot of out-of-town guests, or a big regatta or race such as the Halifax, which occurs every two years, fills all the houses. So why don't more people want to do this? Well, anyone who runs a B & B will tell you it really is a lot of work. More on this in succeeding chapters. The longest-running establishments typically have two people operating them together: a husband and wife, two sisters, etc.

The party my first year was especially fun because it was at my house. Not sure whose idea that was—probably mine. As the living room filled with B & B proprietors, I became aware of an interesting phenomenon: a full measure, almost an excess, of cordiality. These people are people-likers: they have to be—their job involves welcoming people into their houses. The room was overflowing with cries of "How are you?" "You look wonderful!" "How's business?" and the like. The living room was awash in good feeling. They were all so nice they were almost wasted on one other. I've never seen anything like it. Maybe if I'd attended a convention of Power of Positive Thinking graduates. Anyway, it certainly made for a fine party.

And so Marblehead on Harbor was put to bed until spring. I managed to send out an online MoH Christmas card showing the house in the snow, reminding everyone that our next season was just around the corner.

# CHAPTER 5

After the holidays, while things were quiet, somebody—probably Charlie—suggested that it might be a great idea to add a bathroom in a corner of Starboard Home. Not only would it boost business in my best room, it would also free up a dedicated bathroom (on the mezzanine) for the twin bedroom, Amidships. Of course I didn't want to spend the money, and of course I went ahead and did it.

Perhaps Ben's most amazing singlehanded feat was to install this bathroom, out of nothing and all by himself. He removed Larry's empty bureau and took his closet out with a crowbar. We figured we might be able to fit a little corner shower, sink, and toilet in the space. Ben set to work and within a day came to tell me there was enough room for a tub as well. I still don't know how it worked—I suspect witchcraft—but at the end of a week there was a real room coming together there.

"Okay, Becky, put on your skates," said Ben. "We're going to the Homely Depot to pick out tile and fixtures."

Tile and fixtures? I had no idea how to pick out tile and fixtures. As I said, I'm no domestic goddess. I'm not even semi-divine. But I thought maybe a bathroom in light green and cherry red, colors pulled from the bedroom, would be pretty. So Ben went ahead and rounded up a set of tiles in wonderful shades of off-white, taupe, and a warm pinkish brown. Clearly he thought I needed guidance. Bidding adieu in my heart to my color scheme, I let him have his way. Which was much better, considering how small the room was. We moved on and chose Glacier Bay toilet, tub, showerhead, basin, towel bars, and light fixtures. It cost a fair bit, but after the floor tiles were laid, the fixtures slid right into the bathroom as if custom made.

I splurged on a great-looking shower curtain in neutral tones and pale blue, and I bought a rod. I had tons of towels, mostly pale blue and white. It all worked amazingly well.

The final proof of Ben's genius came one morning when he observed, "You know, I think that funny white wicker piece where Larry kept his shirts could fit right into the left corner of the bathroom: it would be perfect for keeping extra paper goods, towels, toiletries, all that stuff." The thing was about five feet high and two feet deep.

"In that tiny bathroom? No it won't."

"Yes it will." Of course it did.

In the basement I found an insanely carved mirror, dark wood and gilt, that Larry had picked up somewhere, and we hung it over the sink. As my brilliant handyman's final gesture, he hung one of the discarded blue, red, and green painted doors from Larry's closet in the bathroom doorway, with doorknobs and a lock. It matched my closet doors, of course, and you'd think the whole thing had been there forever.

I could scarcely believe it. Why hadn't Larry and I ever thought of this? (Probably worried about spending the money.) In the space of just over two weeks, Ben had created a bathroom out of space no one would ever miss. Carpentry, tiling and grouting, electrical circuitry, and plumbing. Plus he was a very cool and funny person. I still have no idea how he led the water from those faraway mezzanine bathrooms to the new one. (Nor do I care.)

I could now advertise Starboard Home as a room with bath ensuite, worth every penny I was charging. The bathroom on the second-floor mezzanine now became the bathroom for Amidships. No longer would there be any issue about sharing with strangers, though people had been sweet about doing so. I was thrilled.

I began getting calls for March and April, and although the house is a little chilly at that time of year, I felt it was worth a try: there were some space heaters lurking in the attic or somewhere. But I made sure potential guests were warned. Several came: the worst didn't happen, the pipes didn't freeze, and everyone was happy.

A young woman arrived one Friday late in March, having booked Seaview. She came downstairs at bedtime to ask me how to lock her door. Having believed that we were all great friends, I had utterly forgotten about locks. Luckily, there was a door key in the top bureau drawer of Seaview that in fact fit the keyhole, so she went to bed safe and, presumably, happy.

The next day I called Charlie. "Do I have to buy locks for the other three bedrooms?" I moaned.

"Mumzi, what are you thinking? Of course you need locks! Furthermore, there should be one on your door and one on the china closet as well, in case people want to lock up valuables." There's no arguing with a newly minted business school graduate. Oh, goody, we get to spend more money.

I called Ben and glumly requested five locks. Ben said he was pretty sure Steerage already had a key in the keyhole. I spent so little time there that I hadn't noticed. So he bought four locks and installed them the next day. And Charlie was right. It made the whole operation look a lot more professional.

A man with a heavy foreign accent called to ask about my statement on the website that "well-behaved children" were welcome. He said he was calling for his wife: they wanted to come for a weekend, but their five-year-old son, Amit, was not well behaved. He was autistic.

"Good heavens—of course, bring him! I won't have any other guests and he can do just as he likes." I was mortified that my thoughtless sanction had made them uncomfortable; I definitely would have to change that.

After our conversation I happened to speak with Charlie.

"Mumz, isn't that Easter weekend? And haven't you invited us all for dinner after church?" Uh oh.

"Is there something wrong with that?"

"Only that you advertise that those rooms are for the guests. You can't suddenly change the rules and kick them out."

"Darn it, of course you're right. We'll have to invite them to join us. But they're Persian: how will they feel about the ham?"

"Never mind. Grab a turkey breast or something."

Bahram and his wife Yasmina came with Amit, who was completely adorable. By Sunday I was in love with the whole family. Amit was better behaved than either of my grandchildren, aged five and three. He tended to twirl on the living room rug on one foot, which was beguiling. The three kids played beautifully together, and the Persian family happily dug into the turkey *and* the ham. And when Charlie and Bahram got to talking, it turned out they were working in the same industry: the garment trade in Israel. Charlie said of all the people he could've met, this man was the most helpful. Strange are the ways of Providence.

I also learned two lessons: first, don't make blanket statements about who's welcome or not, as you may change your mind and you may be doing something insensitive; second, the house isn't really yours, no matter how much you love it, when you have guests. There's a little sting in the second lesson, but I tried not to think too hard about it. The unexpected blessings that had come to us from the sweet Persian family more than made up for it.

Among the other early spring visitors was a group from Connecticut—the staff of a small software development company taking two days off to strategize, build company trust, drop backward into one another's arms, whatever people do on those retreats. It was a new venture for me: there were seven of them spending two nights and two days, and they wanted lunch brought in. I hustled down to the local gourmet store and ordered two menus I thought pretty much everyone would like. I added various teas and some cocoa to the one-cup percolator's offerings and readied both the living and dining rooms for meetings, depending on what they wanted. I also quickly added a sentence or two on the website about how much we enjoyed hosting corporate events.

It went off without a hitch: they had breakfast at the house, of course; I picked up lunch ready to go at the shop; they were on their own for dinner with my notebook of local restaurants to guide them. Since I had ordered too many desserts, I froze them and began gaining back my lost seven pounds. Alas, I never got any more corporate business, but I had fun, and the group added a most enthusiastic message to the guest book.

Late in April a man with a high, slightly grating voice called for two rooms in June: he and his wife were celebrating their daughter's graduation from Boston University, and the three of them wanted to vacation somewhere overlooking the water.

"I've been looking on your website: is Seaview available?"

"It is and it definitely overlooks the harbor," I told him. "And a five-minute walk will get you to Chandler Hovey Park, where there's a lighthouse and a fabulous view of Salem Bay."

"Perfect. Now, your website also says that Steerage can be rented at the same time."

"Well, yes, but who would stay in Steerage?" I was perplexed. The room is quite small, and the threesome were clearly adults.

"My daughter, of course," he answered.

"Mr. Edwards, I really don't think you want to do that. If this is meant to be a treat for your daughter, I wouldn't put her in that room. The name

Steerage says it all. It's just not a great room. I do, however, have a very nice room one floor down with its own bath."

"I don't get it. It says on the website that this is a room for a child."

"Well, yes, but it's appropriate for a baby or a little child, not a grown-up one!"

"She's *our* child! And we'd like to be close together. She'll love that room. It looks great in your picture. We'll take the two."

The camera can lie for promotional purposes, I thought darkly. Wendy's wide-angle lens made Steerage look like a big sunny space instead of the grim little closet it was. I regretted even advertising it. Especially with that picture. I made a note to pull the picture and insist that the room was only an adjunct to Seaview for someone with a baby or a *very* small child.

I called Elaine. "I feel awful for this young lady: here she is, about to graduate from BU, and her father is rewarding her with this lousy room, probably because it's so inexpensive. And I have not just one but two beautiful rooms available. I'm annoyed with Mr. Edwards for being such a cheapskate."

"There's not too much you can do," Elaine observed. "Just try to make Steerage look as nice as possible and hope she's not a drama queen."

When they arrived, I'd done all I could for Steerage: I'd washed the windows, polished the furniture, grabbed the prettiest pillows from the other rooms, and put a large vase of apricot roses on the bureau with a card that said, "Congratulations, Stephanie!" Steerage still looked pretty yucky. I sat back and feared the worst.

Well, of course when you're prepared for it, the worst usually doesn't happen. Stephanie and her parents were on a happy jag and couldn't have cared less about the accommodations. Stephanie was thrilled at having graduated (with a BA in English, Lord help her. I know what that's like), and her parents were overjoyed to have that enormous tuition bill lopped from their budget. As a friend of mine once said, "When it stops, you'll think it's raining money." Stephanie checked out Steerage, admired the roses, and plopped herself down on her parents' bed, which offers a nice view of the beach and the harbor beyond, filling up in late May with boats of all kinds.

"It's amazing! It's awesome! Dad, how on earth did you find this place?"

Dad smiled smugly. You just never can tell.

The Boston Ballet sent a choreography team to the Marblehead-Swampscott YMCA, and called me for rooms. They stayed for a week, giving classes in choreographing to teenagers and young adults at the Y. They brought me the most gorgeous black and Wicked-green t-shirt with a leaping dancer on the front, and I wore it constantly. At the end of their week with me I felt privileged to be invited to see the young people perform the works they had choreographed. It was sensational.

Spring moved into summer and Marblehead on Harbor continued with a number of guests. Just about every one of them was delightful. Jon, a retired professor living in Switzerland, and his wife arranged to meet his brother and wife here: they sat on the porch and I brought them lemonade in the afternoon and wine when I was sure the sun was over the yardarm, whatever that means. After they left, the brother's wife sent me a beautiful little miniature watercolor of the view from their third-floor bedroom, Seaview, which I love.

For my birthday that summer, Charlie gave me a tiny refrigerator that nestled into a corner of the dining room. It made little ice cubes and everything. The guests could put anything from formula and baby food jars to restaurant leftovers, and I wouldn't have to have that stuff in my already-bulging fridge in back. An inspired present.

I had a number of visitors who intuitively grasped the right way to use the house. The Andersons were like that. Three generations: two grandparents, two parents, and their ten-year-old son and eight-year-old daughter. They grabbed a bunch of my beach towels and took off to the little beach across the street—amazingly, although they were from the south, even the parents were able to stay in the cold water for quite a while. Of course the children stayed in until they were blue, and came out protesting that they weren't cold at all. The family ordered cooked lobsters and ate them on the porch around the two glass-topped tables with liberal quantities of Sam Adams summer ale. The children, Robert and Tory, announced they weren't sleeping in Steerage. I couldn't blame them, but when I heard their plan I was aghast.

"We think it would be a lot more fun to sleep on the front porch in the hammock," they told me. "Mom says it's fine if it's okay with you."

"Both of you? It's definitely okay with me: I'm just afraid you won't get a lot of sleep," I demurred. I couldn't think of any sleeping arrangement less comfortable. I assumed that when bedtime came they'd think better of the scheme. But in the morning when I stepped out onto the porch to get the newspaper, I saw a large pile of bedding in the hammock, and, at either end, a mop of curly hair. At breakfast they were bright-eyed and chatty and seemed none the worse for their night out. They slept in the hammock for the rest of their stay.

As the Andersons were leaving, George pulled into the driveway from Lake Winnepesaukee, New Hampshire, with his pretty blond wife Angela. They'd grown up in Marblehead, were childhood sweethearts, and had been married nearly 60 years. Angela was in the last stages of Alzheimer's: all the lights blazing and nobody home. I knew about that and was touched by George's total care for her: a lot of men, maybe most of them, aren't able to cope. She had a shearling coat and hat they'd bought in Tibet that she never took off except when she went to bed, despite the hot July weather.

And over and over she asked George, "Where's Danny?" Danny, I learned, was the family's golden retriever. "Where's Danny? I want to see Danny."

Patiently, he'd remind her that they'd taken Danny to the kennel so they could come to Marblehead and visit their children and grandchildren. She'd acknowledge this, then a few moments later, "Where's Danny?" He was gentle and tender, answering her question each time as if it were new—which to her, of course, it was.

"I used to take Angela out behind the middle school during recess when she was 12 and I was 13," he told me. "She's the first and—believe it or not—the only girl I've ever kissed."

He was a great-looking man, slim and fit despite his age, and she was still a beauty. They must have made a stunning couple in their prime—they were still pretty gorgeous.

Every morning, around 7:00, George would leave Angela sleeping and sit in his Jeep Cherokee smoking and looking at the harbor. I told him he was welcome to smoke on the porch: I think he liked the car radio for company. He ate nothing for breakfast but one English muffin, half a glass of orange juice, and a cup of black coffee. Thus fortified, he'd get Angela up and ready for the day.

I saw him again a year later. Angela had died, and he stayed with me while he and his daughter planned her memorial service. He still got up early and sat in his Jeep smoking and contemplating the harbor. He still had black coffee, an English muffin, and half a glass of juice. He was terribly sad. About eight months later, however, when I saw him again, he was with my live-wire buddy Jane: they'd known each other as couples back in Marblehead days and had reconnected. She tells me that, though it didn't last, they had a wonderful time together. Good. He deserved it.

Marblehead on Harbor, like many new operations, took off fairly slowly, and I really wanted the business. So I took people for just one night, which means lots of beds to change, bathrooms to clean, laundry to process.

I even took a large, crated dog for two nights, though my website said I didn't accept pets. Jay and Jeri came in with a lot of baggage, the crate, and the dog, which was a German Shepherd. I love dogs but am leery of this breed's protective nature. If I reached to carry Jeri's suitcase, the dog might sense a threat and protectively remove my arm. I gave the animal a wide berth, got a firm grip on some twenty pounds of dog supplies, and managed to get all three of them into Starboard Home. The dog, I was glad to see, went willingly into the crate, and the young couple seemed delighted with the room.

I'd asked about any food allergies or diets and been told that Jeri had celiac. Having spent my life with a mother and brother who suffered from this particularly cruel form of gluten malabsorption, I was ready for this. I baked gluten-free cookies and concocted a version of my justly famed breakfast bars that had no wheat germ in it. (This was hard, as the recipe calls for a cup of the stuff.) I baked my regular cookies and bars as well, since I had another couple and their children already booked in. The Jeri cookies went out on the front hall table with a little flag that said "Gluten-Free." The two sets of breakfast bars were ready to go for next morning's breakfast.

In the morning, I carefully flagged the breakfast squares "Gluten-Free" and "NOT Gluten-Free." As I was loading them and the rest of the dishes onto the sideboard, I heard the shower above me. (Starboard Home's newly added bathroom was mostly over the dining room.) The water seemed to be running for a very long time: well, there were two of them. I hoped they weren't washing the dog. Note that I never knew the dog's name—we weren't on those terms. After a while I noticed a spreading stain in the ceiling, with a few drips splashing down onto the dining room rug.

I ran upstairs and knocked on the door. "Hello, Jeri and Jay?"

Jay put his head out the door.

"Tell Jeri to be sure to put the plastic part of the shower curtain *in*side the tub!" I've never understood why this is a problem for some people. Somehow I had correctly guessed Jeri was one of those people.

The dripping had stopped by the time I got downstairs. Another project for Ben up there on my freshly plastered dining room ceiling. At least I was boosting the economy. At least Ben's economy.

Jeri and Jay came down and helped themselves to breakfast. The other couple were Alice and Judy and their two small children from Brattleboro, Vermont, who'd rented Seaview and Steerage. Chatty and cute, they introduced themselves to Jeri and Jay and conversation flowed smoothly. Their children were well behaved and good eaters. My work here is done, I thought, and evaporated into the kitchen.

The group finished breakfast and took off for the day to pursue various amusements. I gave my standard lecture about the places in Salem I felt were good quality (Peabody Essex Museum, House of Seven Gables, and Salem Witch Museum, among others) versus some of the more kitschy spots that simply capitalize on the notorious 1692 witch trials (nameless here forevermore).

As I cleared breakfast, I noticed something disturbing: five wheat-filled breakfast bars were gone; no gluten-free had been taken; and on Jeri's plate were bits of breakfast bar. The inescapable conclusion was that she had eaten a bar from the gluten-ridden batch! What part of "*Not* Gluten-Free" did she not understand? She was going to be feeling ill—right about now. Celiac's revenge for breaking the diet is, for most people, swift and terrible.

My fears were confirmed when the pair came home early, Jeri pale and quiet.

"Did breakfast make you sick?" I asked directly. She nodded.

"Jeri, I am so very sorry: I marked one batch of breakfast bars Gluten-Free, the other not: I wouldn't have done this to you for anything!" She nodded.

"Jay says I took a bar from the same batch as his," she said sadly.

"Oh, dear. Is there anything I can get you?" It wasn't my fault, but of course I felt terrible. And was almost angry at her for making me feel terrible. I had held up my end: she hadn't paid attention.

She had talked me into letting her bring a dog. Now I'd have to practically fumigate the room in case any guests following them into the room were dog-allergic. She had trashed my new dining room ceiling. And now she'd made herself sick! What on earth was *wrong* with her, and why was I feeling so awful about it?

It didn't stop there. The next day they overstayed their welcome by two and a half hours and made me take a thousand pictures of them and the stupid dog. When they finally left, I had to scramble to get the room ready for the couple coming in at three, who mercifully were not allergic to anything. Alice, Judy, and the children had of course left politely at the 11:00 checkout time.

The diet thing was my problem, not Jeri's. I was hypersensitive, because of my family, to doing anything that made a celiac sufferer sick. Memories of Mother and my brother Charlie with the incapacitating cramps and runs the disease causes were ineradicable in my mind. I couldn't help the guilty feelings. On the other hand, Jeri and Jay were a little bit of a pain altogether. You win some, you lose some. Two years later, Jeri called again to rent the room, this time without Jay or the dog. So at least she *thought* she'd had a good time.

Then summer turned to fall, and the leaf peepers started arriving at all the Marblehead B & Bs. I was very busy when this happened. Marblehead, particularly the Neck where I live, usually doesn't get brilliant colors, but it's an easy drive to western Massachusetts, northern Massachusetts, New Hampshire, even Vermont. The leaf peepers typically didn't spend much time with me: none of that rocking on the porch stuff. They wanted breakfast early so they could get on the road. Early for me is 7:00 a.m.—I'm more of an 8:30 girl, but it was their call. I got pretty good at fixing my stepdaughter Liza's Union Square Brunch, a hearty egg and sausage dish I knew would stick to their ribs as they toured.

Among the fall guests were the most touching threesome I met during the entire Marblehead on Harbor experience. Chet called and reserved a long weekend in Starboard Home, the room with the deck overlooking the harbor. He was bringing his girlfriend—and her service dog. Legally I was bound to take them, though because of allergies (and accidents) I advertise that I don't take any animals. I wasn't fighting it: Wendy was blind, and Edward was her guide dog.

They arrived early Friday afternoon. Chet was a huge man in every respect: tall, heavy though not fat, with a booming voice, shaggy beard, and a ponytail like a tumbleweed. Wendy was tiny, with delicate features and a pixie haircut; she dressed in well-ironed cotton skirts and blouses. They treated one another with so much humor and respect that it was lovely to be around them.

Edward, a large golden retriever, was darling: always just the right amount of help for Wendy, but never in the way, clumsy, or overbearing. Like the rest of his breed, he seemed to be always smiling. The couple hospitably invited me to share the deck, which I did. They also stunned me with the news that they were nudists and would be drinking wine in the buff after dark on the deck. You think you've got someone figured out: this emphatically did not mesh with the picture I had formed. They invited me to join them, thoughtfully mentioning that my nudity was optional. I pleaded an engagement in the neighborhood and fled before dark.

Wendy, Chet, and Edward mixed well with the other guests there at the time, none of whom, apparently, were shocked by the nudity going on on the deck upstairs. I can't remember whether anyone was in Seaview, which overlooks the deck: if so, they kept their discoveries to themselves.

Things can run along very smoothly for quite a while, and then something awful happens. One afternoon, complacent with three sets of guests, and having chatted with everyone and assured myself they were going to a nice restaurant, or visiting relatives, or ordering takeout to eat on the porch, I decided to have a fast walk through the neighborhood. As I rounded the corner from Corinthian Lane to Ocean Avenue a car with District of Columbia plates slowed and the driver opened his window.

"Is this Corinthian Lane?" he asked. I looked up: as usual, the bad boys from Boston had stolen the sign. For some reason they think the name is funny.

"Yes, it is," I answered.

"I'm looking for Marblehead on Harbor." Uh oh.

"It's right at the bottom of the Lane, but I'm fully booked for tonight. Did the Chamber of Commerce send you?"

"No. My wife and I have reservations for two nights."

"Are you sure? There are several B & Bs with similar names." I could feel my face flushing and my heart beginning to race.

"If you're Becky, you're the person I reserved with two months ago," said the man. He sounded a little surly. "We've just driven ten hours from Washington, DC; we're tired; and we're looking forward to staying with you in"—he looked at the paper in his hand—"Starboard Home."

This was a double whammy: I could possibly put someone in my bedroom if they weren't expecting a water view and a private deck, but with Starboard Home that doesn't work. The difference between what they expected and what they get is just too great.

"I'm so sorry: Clearly the mistake is mine," I faltered. He just stared at me. What I had done was, I knew, appalling. This couple had driven probably 500 miles to be told there wasn't a room for them. I wished the pavement would open up and swallow me.

"My name is Mitchell Beal." Yes, it did ring a bell—from back in February. I had quite simply forgotten to write the reservation down. An idiotic goof.

"I sent you a check," he continued.

"I can put you up in another, very nice room: I'll refund your deposit, and your two nights will be on me."

"Thanks: I think we'd be more comfortable elsewhere. Just return my deposit." He gave me a final stare, made a U-turn, and disappeared out of my life. I stood there shaking. This was just not okay. It shattered me, and it was absolutely no one's fault but my own.

The attractions of a walk utterly wiped out, I jogged wretchedly back down the Lane. Yes, there was his name in my book, with an address, and the record of his deposit. But why hadn't that translated into a notecard and a spot on the calendar? There was no way of knowing what had distracted me from moving the name onto both when the check had arrived.

Was I losing my mind? Was I just too old for this occupation? It didn't feel good: I felt guilty and ashamed. And I felt incompetent. I'd never heard my B & B compatriots complain about doing this. I was alone, and I was clearly not good at my job. My self-esteem took a bad plunge.

Another bad thought struck. What if Mitchell Beal, with full justification, wrote up this saga on Trip Advisor? He never did. What a nice man.

Eventually I adjusted to having goofed so badly. But it was an important lesson: just keep checking and double-checking that you're not forgetting something important.

# CHAPTER 6

I loved watching the house come back to life. This chapter may bore you, but it's important to me to include the details to show how deeply satisfying it was. There was always something for Ben to do. He, Phil, and Darcy were in and out of the house much of the time. I wasn't alone a lot: this was probably good, though the day I walked into the yard and saw a toilet sitting upright next to the garden, looking ready for use, I was taken aback. Not a good decorating scheme, though it had some practical possibilities. A chat with Ben revealed that the toilet had been literally about to come through the second-floor bathroom floor and the ceiling into the living room! Imagine if you were sitting there in the bathroom minding your business and suddenly found yourself in the living room surrounded by guests—a bad surprise for everyone.

"The floor all the way around the toilet is rotten: it's been leaking water, probably for years," Ben told me. "You have any people coming in this afternoon?"

"Nobody till tomorrow afternoon, actually. Can you have the whole thing back together by then? Two of the guests will be using that bathroom."

"Shouldn't be a problem." Evidently it was. That afternoon I heard shouting and swearing upstairs. Ben and Phil were having a fight. This had happened before and usually ended with both apologizing for their quick tempers and promising eternal friendship. This time, however, Phil ran down the stairs and out the door, still swearing. Ben wasn't far behind.

"That jerk! He thinks he knows more than I do about plumbing," Ben grumbled. He went on for a while about Phil's failings before getting back to work. He managed to get the toilet back in position before the neighbors launched a complaint and well before the guests arrived, but there was no sign of Phil for several days, which was worrisome to me.

Meanwhile, in the yard, a drama was playing out. We'd had a storm, and a tree branch broke loose in the wind and fell into the crotch of the tree, where it dangled dangerously. I called the issue to the attention of Ben. To my eye, the branch looked as if it might fall at any minute. We stood on the porch and took a good look.

"Becky, I'd go up there myself and wrestle that darn branch down, but I'm kind of insecure in a tree. I'm sort of heavy, and I really don't like heights all that much," Ben said.

"I can relate to that," I said. "It might be time to call in a professional. Why don't I phone the tree guy?"

"Probably a good idea." Three was a silence, then Ben suddenly burst out, "If Phil was only here, he'd go right up that tree and cut that branch loose with a knife!"

I stared at him, hopeful.

"You know Phil—he's small, but he's really, really strong. He looks skinny, but he's all muscle. Once I saw him move a Harley Davidson: he just picked it up like it was a can of paint. Darcy said they went to visit friends in New York, but he'll be back early next week."

Unwilling to risk Phil's life and/or the rapprochement I sensed was near, I did call the tree surgeon, who removed the offending branch and made a few other improvements in the line of trees bordering the property. And, as I'd suspected, on Monday Phil and Ben were contentedly cooperating on the Jay and Jeri Memorial Ceiling Leak.

Darcy performed a helpful and unique job on my living room while Phil and Ben were dealing with plumbing problems and such. The living room is painted a wonderful shade of palest salmon pink, achieved at some cost and quite a bit of time a couple of decades ago. We had a painter, Mr. Murphy, who would show up for work at about 5:00 a.m. after a night of who knows what—let's just say the fumes emanating from his body practically intoxicated me. I'd gotten a couple of gallons of paint I thought were the right shade, intending to ask Mr. Murphy to paint a large swatch on the wall. By the time I woke up, the entire living room was finished in an extremely loud between-salmon-and-bubblegum pink. I was aghast: this was not okay. Larry's daughter Liza was visiting.

"Becky, you're overthinking this," she said. "You won't even notice the color once the books are back on the shelf and all the furniture's in place." This was not even close to the truth. I would hate it forever; also it wasn't the vision I'd had, which was one of subtle and surpassing beauty. I was reluctant to let go of that vision.

I went back to the store and asked them to dilute the two cans of paint equally and severely. I did manage to put a swatch on myself, only to discover it was lighter than the Linen White woodwork. That wouldn't do. Back to the store for an injection of color. I went to bed apprehensive, leaving Mr. Murphy written orders to limit his painting to a swatch until I awakened. Mr. Murphy ignored the note and painted the entire room. When I got downstairs, I could hardly believe it: the room was utterly gorgeous and exactly the color I'd seen in my dreams. Round Two to Murphy, and joy all over.

Mr. Murphy's off-pink paint had lasted well for two decades. But over time, the oil heat registers had exuded a dark and greasy residue that had discolored the wall in a number of spots. Ever optimistic, I'd tried to wash it off, which left streaks and also made the surrounding areas look dark and shabby. An effort to match the color and repaint the room had met with no success.

"You can't match dirt," said the mix-master at the paint store. Hurtful but doubtless correct.

I wasn't sure what to do. The room didn't look right, but I loved the color (everywhere it wasn't discolored), which blended so beautifully with the pink and brown majolica lamps, the watermelon-colored draperies, the Oriental rug, and the dark wood of the furniture. What to do?

This is where Darcy's expertise came in. Working with a sponge and who knows what super-gentle cleanser, she was able to remove the dark spots and then blend the clean area in so subtly with the rest of the wall that you couldn't tell anything had been done. It took a while, but the result when she'd finished was dramatic. The room had come alive again. I was thrilled.

Though it was hard to have the handyfolk at work when the B & B was in operation, it was worth it. I felt as if the rooms were at their very best, so I was comfortable charging top dollar (or close to it) for the improved Marblehead on Harbor, of which I was very proud.

# PART TWO

# CHAPTER 7

The B & B sailed along smoothly the rest of that first full season. When I closed shop November first, I had made a terrific lot of money. I loved having the house to myself again: to sleep in Starboard Home, where I'd slept for 37 years; to be able to walk into the living room with a glass of wine, sit down, read a book or work the New York Times crossword puzzle; to have an occasional dinner party; even to let stuff pile up in the public rooms without fearing I might upset the guests. There was in fact one wonderful woman who insisted on visiting in January and taking third-floor Seaview. I put a heater in the room and piled blankets on the bed. She brought me presents and said it was heaven to get away from her mother for a few days. For the most part, however, I was blissfully alone.

While things were quiet, I had time to think, and I then decided I needed to do something about my bedroom—that is, the one I used when I had MoH guests. It had been Charlie's room growing up and had bunk beds with bright blue spreads: Larry and his brother had slept in these beds in the '30s and '40s, and the mattresses were pretty well shot, but I'm a good sleeper and was usually exhausted enough to nod off instantly. The room is on the second floor along with Starboard Home and Amidships and is adjacent to the back stairway (no home is complete without one: show me a child who doesn't love a back stairway and I'll show you a depressed child). This allowed me to pop out of my room and run down that stairway without encountering the guests. Some of them never even knew where I slept, or maybe if. One man thought I slept next door. Most didn't care. That was fine with me.

But I began to feel the room was infra dig for the owner of the B &
B. Charlie had waxed his snowboard on the rug and made a truly revolting mess. The rug was already pretty revolting, being mud-colored and 40
years old. The walls had been painted when Charlie was about six, with
huge, anatomically correct fish: my remarkable friend Carol, an artist, had
taken Charlie's favorite fish from his favorite book, *Fishes of the World*, and
they were gorgeous. She has a talent that's savant-like. I had, however, the
increasing feeling that large creatures with very big eyes were watching
me—eels and anglerfish and other hyperthyroidic entities—and it was a
little disconcerting to get dressed and undressed. It was time for a grown-
up room.

So, early in November, I repainted the room a soft cream color, with
the bright white woodwork I've always loved, and had a Home Depot rug
of a rosy brick-dust color installed wall to wall. I even bought myself a new
queen-sized bed. Ben trotted the bunks up to the attic: the end of an era.
This in no way matched my pattern of parsimony, but I felt I richly (pun)
deserved it. I added ruffled white cotton curtains and a lot of paintings, as
well as photomontages of the children when they were little.

*What a change!* I wrote Connie. *Just walking into my new room makes
me feel wonderful—even, somehow, like a serious adult. And the whole thing
took less than a week!*

One afternoon late in November I called my stepdaughter Mary to
catch up. She lives in Charlottesville and was working her way through a
challenging nursing program, so she wasn't always reachable. This particular day she had time, and we talked for half an hour. The subject of Larry
of course came up: the best dad in the world, we said, and such a good
husband.

I thought about it: he'd been stubborn, difficult at times, stingy with
money, all those things, but I'd had his love and his unquestioning loyalty.

"Speaking of husbands, Becky, when are you going to get yourself
back in circulation?" she wanted to know. I was thunderstruck.

"You mean meet *men?* Mary, come on—it's barely more than a year."

"My point exactly: it's been more than a year."

"I can't imagine it. Your father and I were married for 37 years. It's
hard to picture…dating. Farthest thing from my mind, actually."

"I hate to say this, but you need to get over it. Dad was very practical—when his marriage to Mom blew up, he didn't sit around the house
grieving: he went out and found you. He truly would not want you to bury
yourself."

"But how on earth would I even meet men?"

"What about Match.com?" Mary is divorced and has had fantastic success with this site. Of course it helps that she is young, six feet tall, slim, blonde, and gorgeous.

Interestingly, despite my disclaimers, from the moment she'd brought up the topic, I felt a sort of answering tug. I missed male company, despite enjoying myself enormously with my female friends, going to occasional movies and out for dinner. It might be nice to get a male perspective on things.

"What about Overfifty.com or some site for older people?" I wasn't scared about meeting Mr. Goodbar or anything, but I didn't want to make a fool of myself.

"Match.com," she responded firmly. "There's no comparison."

I let the idea perk for a week or two; then, one afternoon after I'd been playing on the Internet until I felt guilty, I decided to take a look at Match.com. I found myself answering the questions and putting together a profile.

"That's great, Mumz," Charlie said, as he posted some photos that made the most of what's left of my looks. I'm thin and blonde, so I look pretty good in pictures if you're nearsighted enough not to register the wrinkles. Then I sat back and waited.

I didn't have to wait long. Before I knew it, I was eating lunch with several truly nice men my own age. I was amazed. Someone told me that by the time you get to age 70 or so, all the really scary men have been thrown off the site. Or gone to prison or something. The men I was meeting even had reasonably good taste in restaurants. One man, with whom I had lunch at Legal Sea Foods, had a sumptuous garden: he had pictures on his phone. His match name was Sniggi: I learned it was (almost) his last name backwards, which was Higgins. Another had gone to Yale, so I was willing to forgive him his shorts and sandals with black socks. (I'm a card-carrying academic snob.) A third was called Ace, because his family ran the local Ace Hardware store. They were all interesting and lively. In fact, only one of those Match.com meetups was a bomb. The gentleman had brought a portfolio of very impressive photographs he'd taken and discussed them at length. Great length.

"But I haven't even learned a thing about you!" he said, after one of these treatises, then charged off again about his life, career, and photos. When we said goodbye, he observed (accurately) that we probably wouldn't be seeing each other again. On the whole, however, I was having a nice time. But the best was yet to come.

One afternoon I opened up the site to find a message:

"Becky! Est-ce bien toi? It's Toby Sloane!"

I read no further before exclaiming aloud:

"OMG! This could be huge."

I sat there remembering Toby. We had known each other and dated, in a desultory fashion, in our younger twenties. (In those days, you could actually go out with several people at a time. The youth of today have no idea how much fun they're missing.) It hadn't gone far: I was alarmed by his high comfort level teaching and living in a boys' boarding school. And he reminded me of my younger brother. I think also, subconsciously, I was looking at that time for someone to manage me and give me an identity, and this very nice, very young man was just my age and not about to tell me who to be. I already knew Larry, who was just right for the role, with two little daughters, a house, and a business—a genuine grownup in my eyes—so Toby and I had parted friends. I don't know whether he saw me as a life partner either. Probably not. I remembered him, at any rate, as cute, bright-eyed, elegantly slim, and thoroughly charming. Neat and small, with little hands and feet, the latter in shiny loafers. Like an earnest, well-dressed squirrel. When he had visited me and my parents in Virginia, my parents had *loved* him. When we went to church, Mother, watching as he sang from the hymnal, looked as though she might pounce on him and devour him whole. Right there in church. He really did look not only gorgeous, but extremely devout. A little cherub. Just her style.

"C'est moi!" I wrote back immediately and enthusiastically.

*He* wrote back immediately and enthusiastically. "I was in the process of decommissioning the match site. They were sending me a lot of biker chicks. And then they sent me a female impersonator with a peroxide blond wig and black fingernails. It just didn't seem worth it."

I could understand his feelings. But match doesn't want to lose a paying customer, so they continue to send you pictures of people you might like. This was how my face had appeared on his screen.

"But they won't let you contact these people," Toby wrote. "I had to re-up: you cost me $29.95 plus tax."

"I am so worth it," I wrote.

We graduated to phone calls. Amazingly, he called every single night. The first time I heard his voice I was thrilled. It had grown deeper, and his elocution was clear and cultivated and somehow full of possibilities. His vocabulary and the way he used words reminded me in a strange way of myself, which was odd, but nice.

When I admired the voice, he said, "Well, I hate to brag, but for a long time I was the voice of public television for the Connecticut PBS affiliate." Well, that was something to brag about!

It was strange. Missing Larry as much as I did, I was startled by the intensity of my reaction to Toby. And I hadn't laid eyes on him for 40-plus years.

I was going off to Vieques, a small island off Puerto Rico, with several friends from college, but we fixed a date for just after my return. I would be tanned and fit. That was good. We continued to talk and email back and forth. He'd been a widower for a number of years and had taught French and coached crew at a very nice Massachusetts boarding school before retiring about six years earlier. We learned, incredibly, that our children were exactly the same age and had gone to school together—it was astounding that our paths had never crossed. We each had a daughter Sarah (with an h). His other daughter had married a McCauley; my maiden name was McCall. Close enough. Both Sarahs had sons named Charlie. It felt like destiny.

More than this, I fell in love with his writing, which was funny and erudite. Obviously, a French teacher has an interest in words, but Toby loved words in general. In fact, his life seemed to be all about communication: he'd learned Morse code at 12 and was a licensed ham radio operator at 13.

He sounded wonderful from start to finish. He emailed a picture of himself with a little granddaughter on his shoulders. His hair had gone gray, he wore Buddy Holly glasses with thick rims (wholly unfashionable at the time), and his face looked fuller than I remembered, but it was definitely Toby.

During the week in Vieques, which is terrific, especially if you like plantains, I was careful to wish on the first star I saw each night. I did everything I could to get beach gorgeous without overdoing the tan.

"I can't believe how excited I am, and how high my expectations are," I told Elaine as we boarded the plane for home. "How can this miss?" And, I'm embarrassed to say, went on and on. She was nice to listen to my prattling about the upcoming reunion.

When I got back, I called him to confirm the date of his visit.

"I can come up from Barnstable on Thursday," he said. It sounded as though he was planning a day trip, so I replied, "Don't rush off: it's a long way for you to come."

"Fine, but I have to leave on Wednesday at the latest."

Wednesday? Aieee. What on earth was I supposed to do with him for six days?

*       *       *

By the time that Thursday arrived I was pretty keyed up. Toby and I had exchanged many emails as well as talking on the phone, but there was still a lot we didn't know about each other.

Because it was February, I wouldn't have any guests, which pleased me: Toby would see the house the way it was when it was all mine. We could also come and go without running into people, however pleasant and friendly. It would be too cold to sit on the porch, but we could see the harbor from the living room.

Toby called that morning to say he'd probably arrive around three o'clock. I paid extra attention to hair and makeup and put on jeans and a turtleneck and sweater I thought were becoming. Then I sat down on the sofa by the living room window to wait. I got up and walked around. I sat down again. Then I got up again and down again, and I never took my eyes off the road.

Sure enough, at about ten past three a very large red SUV made its somehow stately way down the lane. My heart began to beat extra hard. I'd waited eight weeks to meet this man in person. Now I was so worked up I wished he'd go away. My God, I was behaving like a fourteen-year-old. The doorbell rang. I opened it and was enveloped in a huge hug and an ab-solutely insane burst of conversation punctuated by high-pitched giggles. This was Toby? I stepped back and took a look. In real life he didn't look a bit like the Toby I remembered. He still had that cute little smile and turned-up nose, but he'd developed a large tummy— a very, very large tummy. He was wearing a massive green parka. His face was round and pink. And beaming, actually. He looked like the eponymous hero of "A Visit from Saint Nicholas."

While I took in the new Toby, Toby himself was continuing to talk up a storm. He certainly did have a great voice: I was happy to listen as I adjusted to the new vision of him. We managed to get his bags out of the car and up to his room (Toby still talking the whole time) and I was able to break in long enough to find out that he didn't need anything to eat or drink. Oddly, he never said anything about my house. That sort of hurt my feelings: between the views, the furniture, and all the paintings and collectibles Larry had put together, it's a place that inspires most people to say *something*, even if it's negative. (One man said it reminded him of his grandmother's house. "Right," I said, "And I could *be* your grandmother.") And I loved the house and I wanted him to admire it.

Eventually we established that he'd love to take a walk around the Neck and sightsee. I'm ashamed to report a certain reluctance to let him out in the neighborhood: there are *no* fat people in Marblehead. There may in fact be an ordinance. Seriously, there are very few unfit people in the entire town. Toby had a knee issue, so our walk was slow, dignified, and short.

Afterwards, we had drinks and dinner at home. We talked some more, and I saw him off to bed in Amidships. I called Elaine and in whispers told her, "I have taken into my house a giggling fat boy! What am I going to do?"

Once I'd recovered from the new look, I realized Toby was funny and charming. After all, I sure didn't look the way I had at 22 either. I noted he was not just interested in French words: he loved to play with the English language. He also enjoyed abusing its abusers. Stupid words like *incentivize*, and downright incorrect ones like *irregardless*, made him crazy. So did use of the wrong word: *appraise* for *apprise*, for example. One night he'd called and left me a message mispronouncing the word *efficacious,* as he'd heard on the radio:

"It would be most *effectatious* if you'd call me back." He could, and would, discourse fluently on these subjects. Having taught business English for years and published several books about correct language, I was delighted with this.

I asked him my sphinx rule, which not even my smartest friends had been able to answer: "Why is a crescent moon called a crescent?"

When he answered that it was an *increasing* moon (French *croissant*, growing, from which of course we get the crescent-shaped, increasing moon and, ultimately, the baked goodies), I knew I was beginning to care.

He was also eccentric to a fault. The first morning he came to breakfast in his bedroom slippers. Which is not so bad, except that these were the kind with lots of shearling inside and pouring over the edges so it looks like you're walking around in mashed potatoes. I immediately dismissed the thought that he had any romantic interest in me: would you come down with those on your feet if you were trying to make a good impression? It didn't matter—I was starting to want to make an impression on *him*.

He had a number of funny food quirks, too, starting with a hatred of olives. Olives? Who hates olives?? He didn't like eggplant or any dark green vegetables. And he usually wore a polo shirt with horizontal stripes, which made him look bigger. Why would you do that? He had to have the room pitch black in order to sleep, but he wouldn't wear a mask because he couldn't endure anything touching his face. Sigh. And he invariably slept in his socks (fresh ones for night wear), though I didn't find this out right away.

A history buff, Toby was eager to revisit Concord and Lexington, so that seemed like a good first destination. We toured bridges and battle-fields, and he had so much of interest to say about the towns, the Revolution, its architects, and the poets and writers who had lived there, that I was mesmerized. Over the next few days we went to Walden Pond. We went to Gloucester. I took him to the Peabody Essex Museum in Salem, where he discoursed on the Impressionists. I'm not fond of them, but Toby's interests were starting to develop an aura, so I thought maybe they weren't so bad. We went everywhere within the region.

We ate dinner out one night, and Toby cooked for me one night. This amazed me: I hadn't realized he could cook. In fact, I'd never known any man who cooked. And we went over to *my* Sarah's house in Swampscott on Sunday night to watch the Super Bowl, but really mostly so the family could meet Toby. My little grandchildren were fascinated by him, especially by his size. He took it well.

"How much do you weigh?" asked little Charlie, round-eyed.

"Oh, about eight hundred pounds, more or less," Toby replied. The children gasped. I was liking him more and more.

Tuesday, the day before he had to leave, Toby was chopping celery at the kitchen sink for chicken salad. I stepped up to the cutting board beside him to chop chicken. We were talking, and he straightened up, turned to me, and kissed me on the lips. Just a light kiss. I realized that, until that moment, I hadn't really been sure what he had in mind. It was good to know.

That night after dinner we watched a little TV; then I built a fire in the living room and offered him some brandy and a seat on a little sofa facing the fire. I sat down beside him in my favorite dress with some vague idea of seduction in mind. Some kisses and a little more ensued, then I suddenly said, "I'd better stop—I have absolutely no idea what I'm doing."

It was true. I guess after you've been married to one person for many years, you get pretty much out of the dating thing. I didn't know what to do or expect. Toby had had, maybe two years earlier, just one slightly un-happy relationship since his wife had died. Between the two of us, then, we had very little experience in building new relationships. As the guy tells Tom Hanks in "Sleepless in Seattle," "I bet you don't even know what tiramisu is." I wasn't even sure, for example, since he'd been visiting for six days, whether we'd had one date or six, and how far one was expected to go, intimacy-wise, in either case. Now they tell me there is no such thing as a date. Aieee.

The next morning, as I went down the front stairs, I saw the two pictures of Larry I'd hung many years earlier, which made me feel sort of guilty for my growing feelings for Toby. In one of the pictures Larry's showing a bunch of rather small fish he's caught. He has the biggest, happiest smile on his face. In the other, he's standing in a shallow forest pool in his bathing suit at the bottom of a rock slide. With one hand, he's holding on to six-year-old Sarah, sputtering in the pool; he's holding out his other hand to our little Charlie, four, encouraging him to get up his courage and jump in. I felt my eyes fill up: what a father they'd lost.

The 15-year age difference between Larry and me had been good for me in many ways, but it had meant that the children had lost a wonderful father at a relatively young age. The photograph was a metaphor of his tender care for all of us. Looking at it, I questioned the rightness of my present happiness. Then I remembered Mary's take: Dad wouldn't want you to bury yourself. Get out there! Well, I was out there, all right.

When Toby left after a quick breakfast, I saw his car out of the driveway and waved till he was out of sight.

When he got home, I got an email that said in part: "Becky, I am so dizzy-dazzled by you. I love you. Toby."

I had surely never dizzy-dazzled anyone before. And he said he loved me! It felt wonderful.

# CHAPTER 8

The next logical step was for me to drive down to Barnstable for a weekend. Toby said that if I got through Boston by 12:30, I'd be okay with the commuters. Vacationers on Cape Cod were not a problem, as it was only the beginning of March.

I wrote Connie:

> *Good grief, I am so happy. Happy and excited! I'm looking forward to seeing Toby more than I've looked forward to anything in years. I've packed all the prettiest clothes I haven't already worn for him. I wouldn't trade places with anyone on earth. XXOO Much love.*

She wrote back:

> *Take it easy, say I. Remember the line from* Romeo and Juliet: *"These violent delights have violent ends." I don't want you to have a violent end. Much love.*

I had work to do in the morning before I could leave. I had scored a gig coaching a German CEO in Andover, helping her with writing and speaking English. Hannelore ran a company that employed 400 people. She also played the clarinet in a band that entertained at weddings, bar mitzvahs, and various other observances. And she was fairly young and quite pretty. And incredibly smart, with a frank and incisive take on things, probably including me. I have had a lot of experience teaching business English, both to classes and one on one, but I was beyond intimidated by her: I was scared to death.

I have to admit it was an interesting experience, though, and I learned a lot about why English is so hard. Do you realize, for example, that the word "have" is pronounced in two distinctly different ways? Compare "I *have* four pens" and "I *have* to leave now." See? Your German grammar book probably doesn't tell you that; at any rate, it hadn't told Hannelore, who would say with impunity, "I haff only one hour today." For her part, being a successful businesswoman, she was not defensive about what she didn't know. People like that are good to coach. But I was nevertheless often frightened to the point of incoherence.

The day I was driving down to Barnstable I had a session with Hannelore, but this time it felt different, because at the end of the session I would see Toby. My heart felt as if it would jump out of my chest. If I felt a pang of nerves at the thought of Hannelore's stony stare, I had only to think of the reward awaiting me on Cape Cod.

That morning, I was trying to explain to her why we don't say "process-*eez*" (although many poorly informed people do). Hannelore had said it, and I was in the process of trying to stamp it out.

"That '-es' ending, which we pronounce 'eez,' is reserved for nouns that end in '-sis'—this includes basis, thesis, crisis, diagnosis, words like these. Why do you think we drop the '-is' and replace it with '-es'?"

"I can't imagine."

"Come on, Hannelore! You can do this. What would you have if you made an ordinary plural out of 'basis'?"

After a short think, Hannelore said, "You would say 'basises.'" (I told you she was smart.)

"Anything wrong with that?"

"Well, it is a lot of esses."

"Exactly!" I crowed. "It's pretty unwieldy, isn't it?"

"It wouldn't bother me, or anyone else who speaks German. We are used to the—what do you call it?—unwiedly."

"Unwieldy. You make a good point. But somebody or other in authority decided it was too much for us poor English speakers, and made this rule. It does not, however, apply to just any noun that has an -s on the end. Process, stress, and bus all end in -s but not in –is. Do you have any questions about this?"

She seemed happy with it, but I still wonder whether she kept on saying "process-*eez*" in meetings. There are a number of people who believe it sounds learned. Oh, well: you do what you can.

The hour and a half ended, and with mutual professions of esteem, we parted, Hannelore to terrorize her staff, I to jump in the car, Cape-bound. I set up Siri to head for Toby's house and burned rubber out of the parking lot. It was a sunny day, mild for March, and I felt Nature was on my side. They call that the Pathetic Fallacy: Nature isn't. Frankly, Nature doesn't give a damn. But just knowing I was going to see Toby had me on top of the world: It could've been raining and blowing a full gale and I would still have been joyful.

I'd had an email from Elaine that morning which read,

*I thought he was a giggling fat boy and you were writing him off. Where is all this enthusiasm coming from? Or does it turn out that you have a thing for GFBs? Love, Elaine*

I can't explain the feeling I had for Toby: it had developed in part over the weeks when we'd known each other only by phone and email. We had discovered that we were actually very good companions and had more in common than our children's names and schools. The language thing was, of course, huge. We shared a fairly conservative take on politics. We both loved music of just about every kind. His choices were my choices, and neither of us was pretending. I'd email him, for example, the words from the movie "Babe" to the Saint-Saens organ symphony theme. He'd send me his favorite recording, on YouTube, of the carol "In the bleak midwinter." And so on.

But it had its roots much further in the past. I think he represented youth, and beauty, of long ago (both his and mine), and parental approval, and a feeling of coming home to something deeply familiar. Something even slightly Southern. (I'm originally from Virginia, the heart of the South and capital of the Confederacy.) I had even made my peace with his weight, and I barely noticed the giggling. I thought also that I could probably get some of that weight off: then I'd be able to see once again that lovely boy I'd known.

To say I was in love hardly begins to explain it. I drove south in a happy dream. When I arrived in Barnstable and found my way to his house in the woods, we flew into one another's arms like something in a movie (a bad one). As Toby showed me around, each room seemed suffused with charm, as if haloed. That's *amore*. The sun poured into the dining room and the study. The laundry room had a wonderful spicy smell. The kitchen was tidy. He had four bedrooms upstairs, small, but cheerful with color-ful quilts. He had a large deck on the back side of the house with several bird feeders, which he said attracted some noteworthy birds. It gave onto a forest, and it got dark early in the afternoon. When I was in grade school, I had a wonderful science teacher who made birds come alive for me. In fact, he once had his students lie down in a field, "To attract vultures." As we lay there, he tiptoed away. Anyhow, I liked birds and was delighted to see Toby's feeders.

"Are you interested in birds?" he asked.

"Yes. My father knew all the birds in Virginia, and their calls. I wish I'd paid more attention."

"My mother too. She once flew to the Galapagos to find one of the last birds on her life list!"

"Please tell me she had other reasons to fly to the Galapagos." I like birds, but that was verging on obsessive.

"Not sure. I was married with kids and very busy."

When he spoke about his marriage, I felt a little sad and a fair bit jealous. This didn't make much sense, of course, since I'd had a husband and children as well before Toby came back into my life.

Might as well get into it, I thought. "What was your wife like?" I asked.

His answer came quickly: "She was incredibly well organized. I'm not, so we made a good team. She had lists, and lists of lists, and if she took on a job, big or small, it was always done really, really perfectly."

It seemed a funny thing to think of first when you survey a long-term marriage. But every marriage, every couple, every person is different.

"She was practical, too," Toby went on. "She bought us a plastic Christmas tree so we could use it year after year. And she loved to read."

"What kind of books did she like?"

"Romance novels. She loved them, especially Harlequin Romances."

Aieee. To say I felt less jealous is putting it mildly. Poor Caroline—and Toby didn't even seem to be aware that what he was saying wasn't making her sound very appealing — to me, at least. Well, as I said, every person is different and so is every marriage.

Thinking about what Toby saw as the salient features of his wife's personality, I began to see that Caroline might have had a difficult marriage, even maybe a somewhat difficult life. Pickled as he was in the strong brine of numerous boarding schools, Toby would have found nothing strange about the way they lived, where everything was taken care of for them. But Caroline could have been sincerely put off her game. The incredible organization, making list after list, could have been a control thing. I mean trying to get her arms around an unfamiliar situation—possibly she felt out of control with the school paying Toby little but offering almost intrusive perks, such as repainting her living room, or taking the car for inspection. At their convenience, probably. All in your point of view, but maybe she didn't like it. The plastic Christmas tree? Economizing, for sure. I knew about that. As for the romance novels, that's the kind of thing I turn to when I really need to escape my present situation. I not only felt less jealous of her; in fact, I felt the stirring of sincere sympathy.

We took a brief walk around Toby's neighborhood. It was very quiet: a lot of the houses were second homes, used only in the summer. That meant little traffic and less noise, which was nice. Toby cooked a lovely dinner of lamb chops and mashed potatoes. There was hugging and kissing on the sofa and we watched an old movie, "Dead Poets Society." I love Robin Williams (may he rest in peace) and had seen the movie twice, but it was made more interesting by the fact that it had been filmed at one of the schools where Toby had taught. He even showed me his classroom. When the movie ended, and I had dried my eyes, I was put chastely to bed in the guest room.

"May I come in and wake you in the morning, cherie?" Toby asked.

"You bet," I said happily. "I love you."

The next morning he came in and slipped into my bed. I was just waking up and felt almost ill with happiness. We tussled about a bit before heading down to breakfast. I spent the day in a daze: I was pretty sure I knew what the night would bring. When we went out for dinner, I couldn't help noticing Toby looking at me like something on the dessert menu. I tried to keep up a witty conversation; it went only so well.

"That man over in the corner has eyes for you," he leaned forward and whispered to me.

"I truly doubt it. He's seeing a 68-year-old woman."

"So am I."

"Maybe you're seeing me the way I'm seeing you—as a 23-year-old."

"Let's go home."

I had a tardy pang of guilt and fear. How was this going to go? Was I being somehow untrue to Larry? I knew that was nonsense. It was probably mostly nervousness and fear of the unknown.

There was no need. It was lovely, and tender, and easy. I slept a deep sleep with wonderful dreams. And there, in the morning, was Toby.

"I love you so much it hurts!" I told him.

Toby answered, "I love you so much, and it feels great!"

And then one night during the weekend, Toby said sleepily, "We could get married."

My breath caught in my chest. A proposal! Stupidly, I said the first thing that came into my head: "But where would we live?" We were both so clearly and deeply attached to our homes.

Toby answered, "Some people get married first, and worry later about where they're going to live."

Well, okay. Anyway, it gave me an idea of where we were headed with this. But I was a little worried, because as much as I loved Toby, I couldn't see myself leaving my house for his. Would I have to sell mine? That landed me right in the middle of Teardown City. Maybe I could persuade him to come to Marblehead. Anyone would want to live at #15, I thought. Though he hadn't seemed particularly smitten. I guessed over time we could work it out.

We visited back and forth over the next couple of months, MoH being still closed. I missed my house, its warmth and wonderful paintings, its quirky charm. Toby's house, I realized, had very little of the personality of mine—just a fact—and it got dark early in the day. But Toby was in it. I still liked it better when he came my way: the house seemed to welcome him.

The Boston Globe reported that a bird called the lazuli bunting, rarely seen in this region, had apparently gotten lost in a storm on its way to Mexico for the winter, and was consequently wintering over at the Audubon Sanctuary not too far from Toby. With a name like that, I figured it would be colorful and beautiful. So the next time I was in Barnstable, we drove over to see it. There was a big area with a glass wall facing us, and we were told the lazuli bunting was in there. We spoke to some people who'd been waiting for him for several hours—there was quite a crowd. They had begun to wonder whether he was coming!

We were lucky. After less than a half hour, suddenly the place exploded: people were whipping out cameras and adjusting tripods. We'd been told this bird was a ground feeder, so we looked down and there he was, sort of sauntering along, looking pleased with himself. I was so excited I forgot to take a picture—I think Toby got a few. The lazuli bunting, like many things, was perhaps not quite as beautiful and thrilling as billed, but because we had found him together, he and the enterprise were special. Like everything we did, the bunting acquired that special aura.

In April, Toby's cousin Frank and his wife Andy came to the Cape for a few days. We met them for lunch in Chatham. It was fun to see Frank, whom I'd actually known in Virginia years and years earlier, and Andy was lovely. After we'd said goodbye, Toby put an arm around me and whispered, "Andy wanted to know when I'm going to make an honest woman of you!" We laughed. But I realized that I was a marrying sort of person: this sounded very good.

# CHAPTER 9

Spring came along, and it was back to work for me. I had quite a few guests lined up for my second season, and though I was excited to meet them, I realized Toby and I had enjoyed an idyll that wasn't coming round again for a while. We'd spent a lot of time together while winter had closed the doors of Marblehead on Harbor, and I was somewhat concerned that he hadn't yet experienced the phenomenon of having guests around, nor had he shown any interest in doing so. I couldn't blame him: running a B & B isn't for everyone. But I was feeling a loss. Somehow I'd thought he would like to help me at least a part of the time.

On the other hand, it was always an adventure to meet the guests: as Forrest Gump's mother said about a box of chocolates, you just never know what you're going to get. Every time the door opened, there was a new and usually fascinating story.

Four ladies having an informal college reunion arrived early in the season. "The cold won't bother us!" Jenny had insisted over the phone when she was making the arrangements. Humph. They were from eastern Pennsylvania and Delaware—what did they know about cold? Fortunately, it was mild. I planned several especially nice breakfasts for them, and opening up put me in a good mood. My enthusiasm was dampened, however, when Jenny took me aside: "Adele is Jewish: she can't eat bacon." Of course I apologized immediately and profusely, but how was I supposed to know she was Jewish when no one had told me? For the rest of the weekend I cooked as if everyone were Jewish. They left with enthusiastic messages in my guest book—even Adele—and sent me a doughnut-making kit.

When some but not all of the thousands of boats were back in the water, I had two of my favorite guests ever: a father and son from Colorado, both named Matthew, on a Cape Ann to Cape Cod coastal painting vacation. The father had a neatly trimmed beard and short, graying hair, the son a long blond ponytail and a free-range beard. They ate well, drank iced tea on the porch, and were generally perfect guests. They were heartwarmingly pleased with the harbor view, which they painted many times. One morning I came out to find Matthew the younger doing a seascape while Matthew the elder, a finger to his lips to ensure my silence, surreptitiously did his son's portrait in charcoal.

A statuesque redhead, beautifully dressed and turned out, breezed in from New Jersey. She was accompanied by what I could only assume was a genuine Hell's Angel. He had liquid, dark eyes and a fuzzy, grizzled beard and ponytail, a black T-shirt with the Harley logo in gold, black chinos, and black boots open to the instep. An interestingly assorted pair. They had driven up in a sedate Chevy sedan, the motorcycle doubtless in the shop being fitted for new killer wheels. Kathleen was on her way to see her doctor at Mass General in Boston. She told me that after donating a kidney to her sister a year before, she hadn't had a single day without pain. This is something no one at the hospital shares with you: surprisingly, it's often much harder on the donor than the donee. Poor lady! That's what you get for doing something saintly. And to think that I'd volunteered to donate a kidney, not once, but twice. (I was rejected for being too old, which seemed unkind, but maybe I'd dodged a bullet.)

The next day, at breakfast, I couldn't keep my eyes off the two of them. They were my only guests that morning and the incongruity between them was startling. I had made a lovely bacon and spinach quiche, which Mr. Motorbike was wolfing down as if there were no tomorrow. Kathleen must have seen my amazement, for she launched into their story. She'd been married to a man who had developed multiple sclerosis and was confined to a wheelchair. An attentive and painstaking nurse, she took great care of him herself, had a regular guy come in to do heavy chores for him, and felt they were managing well. One day while she was out grocery shopping, he managed to get into the shower and hang himself. She came home, found him, and was hysterical with grief and guilt.

"Oh, my God," I breathed.

"I called 911 and the ambulance came. I also called his dearest friend, the best man at our wedding. He jumped on his motorcycle and came roaring up from Florida. And," she added, "He never left." These two people, however different, had surely been drawn together by their love for a dead man and their shared sense of loss.

A man and a woman arrived from Maine and New Jersey, respectively. They said they were both divorced and now a couple. They vanished into Starboard Home and I literally didn't see them for two days. When they left, I found four of those big, *big* wine bottles empty beside the wastebasket. It looked as if they'd had a good time. An assignation? I wasn't so sure about those divorces.

Summer arrived and I fell in love with a gay couple from Savannah, Tom and Peter. Middle-aged and clearly devoted, they fussed at each other constantly—Peter particularly giving Tom the needle for his disorganized behavior. Tom, a gentle soul, put up with it—though I suspected he wasn't as drifty as Peter claimed. They were obviously very smart people, discussing politics and Victorian poetry with equal ease: they were a lot of fun.

After they'd been with me for two nights, they insisted on taking me out for dinner. I protested.

"This isn't right: I'm supposed to be treating you, not vice versa."

"We want to take you to the best restaurant in town."

"But why?"

"Because you're nice to us."

I thought about how much unkindness they'd certainly endured. I hadn't gone overboard being good to them: they were just asking to be treated decently. Of course I couldn't resist such company: we went to a lovely restaurant and had a bang-up time. The restaurant was one at which Peter had been a busboy in his teens: much nostalgia ensued.

They left two days later in a great uproar, Peter nagging Tom incessantly about all the stuff he was surely forgetting. They drove off with Tom leaning out the window shouting, "Bye-bye, Miss Becky!" He pronounced it "Bah-bah." I waved madly.

I discovered they'd both left their cell phone chargers behind (everyone does it), but Peter had also left his entire travel kit. As I wrapped their stuff for mailing, I couldn't help hoping Tom would score a few points off Peter for a change.

Cindy and Rick arrived to visit his father in Marblehead. They were young and full of enthusiasm. Rick was one enormous smile and a ton of jokes. Cindy was all smiles as well and as the result of surgery had a long steel rod imbedded in her leg from her thigh to her ankle, leaving her with absolutely no mobility in that leg. Since no one had mentioned any problem with mobility, I had given them the Seaview bedroom on the third floor, with the bathroom seven steps down. This was not going to do—but the rest of the rooms were taken. I moved out of my bedroom and let them stay there: fewer steps to the bathroom and only one staircase to get to the room instead of two. As for me, I spent five sleepless nights on the lumpy sofa bed in the kitchen area, the Chelsea clock chiming madly every half hour. They were worth it. Rick obviously adored Cindy and was tremendously solicitous of her. But he talked her into going on a whale watch! I was astounded: How could someone with three feet of steel in her leg get onto and off one of those boats? She was game for most anything, obviously. They were lovely to have around.

Tina and Ernest came from Santiago to attend a wedding at Castle Rock. It was to be a small one, which was good: sometimes the guests get excited taking pictures on the rock, and I'm always scared if there's a crowd that someone's going to go over. I tried to talk to Tina about the wedding. It was her nephew, her brother's son, who was being married. She seemed oddly reticent, so I backed off asking for details about the bride's outfit, who was to be in the wedding party, and so forth. Maybe a language issue. She did show me what she was planning to wear, which I thought was lovely and appropriate and told her so. She responded by tearing up. Well, I thought, weddings tend to bring on these emotions, but it seemed a little strange, and sad.

The afternoon of the wedding arrived, my guests got themselves dressed up at quarter to four and marched out my door—Castle Rock is only a couple of blocks away. The reception was to be held at Tina's brother's house. Tina and Ernest arrived back at about eight o'clock.

"How was it?" I'd come out of the kitchen when I heard them, hoping to hear about the wedding. "Was the bride gorgeous?" Easy lob: Brides are always gorgeous.

Ernest hemmed and hawed a little. "We need to tell you: there isn't any bride, actually," he said. "Tina's nephew married his boyfriend of several years. A lot of our relatives, even those who live nearby, refused to attend the wedding. It's been pretty tense."

"Well, I'm happy for them. And I'm proud of Massachusetts for passing the law that allowed them to marry," I replied. "My nephew down in Virginia is gay: he and his partner of ten years are waiting for the law in Virginia to change so they can be married there."

Tina burst into floods of tears and threw herself into my arms. Sweet lady, she'd been carrying a heavy burden, and my comments hadn't helped at all. (Note to self: don't assume there's a bride and a groom on every wedding cake.)

"Tina is a very good Catholic: she was so afraid you'd judge us for supporting them."

How touching that Tina gave a hoot what I thought. And she sends me a Christmas card every year.

# CHAPTER 10

My late husband Larry never cared for screens, feeling they cut down on light and the view, and I feel the same way. As a result, we never put any up. As a further result, we sometimes got unwanted visitors. One afternoon while hosting the B & B, I opened the side door to unwind the flag, which had, as usual on windy days, wrapped itself around the flagpole, and a nondescript small bird flew in.

"Hey!" I yelled. "Get out of here!" I had guests coming in two hours (assuming I was lucky and they didn't show up early, as often happened), and I had better things to do than to chase a feathered intruder around the house. In fact, I had beds to make and floors to vacuum. The bird, failing to get the concept, flew up the stairs.

I raced up behind him. He swooped around the second floor, occasionally dropping a calling card, batting his wings furiously the whole time. Finally I managed to chase him into my bedroom and shut the door. Then I completed my preparations for the guests.

When everything was ready for their arrival, I turned my attention back to the bird.

I slipped into my bedroom, opened a window to its fullest extent, and tried to chase him out. He went under the queen-sized bed. I crawled toward him, forcing him to move. He began flying all over the room, frustrating my every attempt to aim him toward the window. I got a towel out of the linen closet in the corner and tried to catch him in it. Finally I gave up. He acted as if it were a game. I left a saucer of water and some crackers on the bureau: I didn't want him to die of hunger or thirst. It was sort of my fault he was there—if I'd been like other people, I would have put up at least a few screens.

I checked in a pair of new guests, saw them off for dinner, had my own, then got ready for bed. I'd sort of forgotten the bird. I was forcibly reminded when I opened my bedroom door to be greeted by a battery of wings. He had pooped on my bureau; when I mopped it up, I saw it had taken the finish off. Nice. After chasing him around the room for a while, I decided we could share the bedroom for the night. This was a bad decision: he spent the entire night swooping around the room, beating his wings against ceiling, windows, and walls. I got almost no sleep and was utterly bleary when the alarm went off at 6:30, signaling that it was time to make the pancakes. I left him to it and went down to feed people.

The rest of the day I left him shut in the room, windows wide open should he choose to use them. He didn't. The second night passed much like the first, perhaps a little calmer. When Toby called, I was almost tearful. Despite being such a bird person, he had no new suggestions. He was, however, very sympathetic, and promised that when he came up the following weekend, he'd have a go at Mr. Little Brown Bird. This wasn't very comforting, since it was only Monday.

The bird went under the bed again next morning after I'd cleaned up breakfast, and I followed. I took something delicious, a snack bar or something, and offered it to him. He put his head on one side and looked at me, I thought, as if he was amused. That made one of us. I suddenly saw myself as he or anyone else might see me: an elderly lady lying full length on the rug with a candy bar, trying to charm an expletive-deleted bird who was ruining her sleep and her quality of life. It was humiliating.

I briefly considered some kind of spray that would impair his ability to fly, such as hair spray, but it seemed so brutal I gave it up. Then, out of the dim, distant past, I had an inspiration. I stood at the foot of the bed with a towel in my hands and began to whistle. I then kissed the back of my hand: the Audubon Society, a million years ago, used to tell us that birds liked the sound. Amazingly, he stopped flying and stood on the pillows, again looking at me sideways. Then, very slowly, he began stepping toward me.

I'd learned something in the last two days, so I didn't rush into anything. I just stood there, more or less immobile, making my little whistling and kissing noises. Eventually he reached the foot of the bed. I leaned forward slowly and enveloped him in the towel. He didn't even make a peep. I took him over to the window and let him go. From the way he soared into the sky, never once looking back, you'd think he'd been dying to leave the entire time instead of hanging around my room making a nuisance of himself.

I'd wasted the better part of two days trying to deal with the dratted bird. And now I was afraid to open the outside doors in case another dim-witted animal decided to make my house its home. Suddenly I felt very tired and a little disgusted. This was no way for a woman with a graduate degree to make her living. I stomped on the thought and went about my chores.

When Toby arrived for the weekend, he had a net. Though I no longer needed it, I was touched: You have to love somebody who goes out and buys a net because his girlfriend is entertaining a bird.

In late afternoon, we walked up to the lighthouse to watch the boats come in from their various races. We sat on a backless granite bench near the edge of the little cliff which sloped steeply down to a rocky beach. After a few minutes, Toby straddled the bench, turned me sideways, put his arms around me and held me from behind. A beautiful sunset was beginning: delicate pinks and blues were coloring some puffy fair-weather clouds. We watched the boats coming into the harbor.

"I will love you forever," Toby said.

"I will love you till the twelfth of never," I answered. Could I have been any happier?

# CHAPTER 11

As the summer progressed, the B & B became more popular, and guests continued to appear. Have I mentioned the phenomenon of the hugging wives? Any number of women, when they arrived in my driveway and I ran out to get the luggage, would come racing up the walk to give me a big, big hug. I didn't mind, but I found it puzzling. Have we met?

I figured it out eventually. Many people landed at Logan Airport, rented a car, and drove north to Marblehead. If you're familiar with the area, you know you'll be driving through some fairly heavy afternoon traffic and some fairly blighted real estate: the parts of East Boston, Revere, and Lynn of which these areas have least reason to be proud. I guessed that as they rolled down the Lynnway, a long streak of used car lots, abandoned motels, and dollar stores, the average husband, tired and cranky, is probably saying something like: "Tell me again, Marjorie. Where did you find this gorgeous bed and breakfast? In the Yellow Pages? Mad Magazine? The neighborhood is *so* lovely." And so forth. And then they hit Swampscott, with the ocean on the right, and things begin looking up. Then Marblehead, which is really very pretty. And finally down Corinthian Lane, where he can see on his right a big white house with a flag, and on his left, about a thousand boats afloat. Instant happy husband. The wife, as you can imagine, is now feeling extremely positive about Becky. The relief! The enthusiasm! No wonder there is a lot of hugging and air kissing.

There was actually one very cute hugging wife from San Antonio, Texas, who turned the whole experience into a visit to a friend: she had brought me hostess presents, a very upscale bottled set of oil and vinegar and a beautiful leather purse. Well, I would be the last person to tell her she didn't need to do this.

The Boston Ballet choreographers returned for their gig at the YMCA. I was thrilled to see them again—young, animated, and beautiful. Because they were dancers and needed to stay in fabulous shape to demonstrate moves and set a good example, they all ate very carefully, mostly vegetarian; fruits and nuts were popular. They stayed strictly away from anything that resembled bread. There was one exception to this strict regime: They put more sugar and cream in their coffee than you can believe. I had to refill the sugar bowl three times in a week for them—usually it sits on the table, lonely and ignored. I guess this is the way they kept going—otherwise they would've collapsed from lack of energy and near-starvation.

Helen came for the Ballet week both times. I discovered by accident how well known she is. I saw her name in the New Yorker not long ago: the article said something like, "If you have a choreographer the likes of Helen P__...." I was dazzled. To think this lady, my B & B guest, was the standard of choreographic excellence—and in New York! She was great company, too. An early riser, she disregarded all the signs on the doors into the kitchen that said "Private," helped herself to coffee, and came and sat with me while I churned out the breakfast fare. Anyone would've loved her, and I did.

I almost never had a guest I didn't warm to. But in July a couple from Rhode Island came for a local wedding. They eyed their surroundings unappreciatively and quickly earned the ire of the other guests, who found them unresponsive to the point of rudeness. The wife, beautifully turned out even at breakfast, with dark hair that flipped like Dear Abby's, exchanged glances with her husband and emitted a snarky little giggle at every comment any of us made. Her husband, an ambulatory cliché in navy blue blazer, Nantucket reds, and Topsiders—only the Mount Gay Rum hat was missing—said and did nothing except eat breakfast: lots of it, though in a well-bred manner. His wife had told me when they arrived that he would have a three-minute egg for breakfast each morning. I told her MoH wasn't that kind of place. She didn't like it.

It didn't help that one of the other guests managed to be at the same time the sweetest and most charismatic woman you could ever hope to meet; she had me enthralled from the moment she came in the door. Laura was a pharmaceutical rep who'd come to Boston for a conference. She had some wonderful ideas for gifts for two guests visiting their cousins; she gave me a terrific recipe for pumpkin muffins; she even suggested several medicines for insomnia, which we all appreciated and which I passed on to poor sleeper Toby.

Of course, Laura's warmth made the snooty wedding guests appear even more annoying. Every morning after they left the table, the group sat around thinking up reasons why they disliked Mr. and Mrs. Westerly so intensely and what they should do about it. They appealed to me to join the fun. This was hard for me: I agreed with them but felt it wasn't right for me as the B & B proprietor to hurl the envenomed dart. And I managed to cut off a short-sheeting expedition at the pass.

Mrs. W. had brought a beautiful apricot and white chiffon dress for the wedding and asked to use the iron. As she came into the kitchen I exclaimed over the loveliness of the outfit, but couldn't resist cautioning her against applying too much heat. She responded airily that the steam from the iron would keep it cool. I busied myself at the sink and awaited the inevitable. Sure enough, iron and dress became quickly bonded. Everybody knows you can't put a hot iron on chiffon. Fortunately, the outfit featured so much swirly material that the damage was easily hidden. But the roar that went up after they left and I told the tale was deeply expressive. (Laura tried to say something kind but was shouted down.) It's a great feeling to satisfy a group of people so thoroughly.

A German couple arrived on a Tuesday, staying until Friday morning. They gave me Guten Tag. I replied in kind, using up two of my ten German words. It transpired they spoke just about zero English. I felt bad for them. I was once in student housing in Istanbul where no one spoke English, and the desk clerks evidently didn't understand the way I was pronouncing the words in my Turkish-English pocket dictionary. It's a scary feeling. I couldn't help wondering why they had come to me. I was soon to find out.

With a great deal of difficulty and using *his* pocket dictionary, the husband told me the website claimed that German was spoken at my B & B! What on earth?

"Ich spreche keine Deutsch! So sorry, the website is…nein, nein, nicht wahr." Then, with a dawning suspicion, "Mein sonne spreche Deutsch!" Charlie, having almost flunked, in succession, French, Spanish, and Latin, took up German in his early twenties. It seems like a miracle to me, but he is very good at it. Well, there wasn't anything good about this caper.

I went straight to the website and sure enough, read a new paragraph: a mother and her son run Marblehead on Harbor together, and German is spoken there. Unbelievable! I called Charlie and gave him a serious piece of my mind.

"You miserable little wretch! What were you thinking? You get on the phone and talk to this poor couple!" I said, when I had finished pointing out to him how unfair this was to the Bergers. It was also, for that matter, false advertising. "See if there's anything they want that they don't have. I've half a mind to make you come out here and fix them breakfast!"

"Mumzi, I'm sorry! I got a little carried away a few months back when I thought I'd have more time away from work and could actually come help you. Do you need me to come out?"

"Well, maybe not, if you can just chat a bit with them: apologize and tell them to call you if they encounter any problems. I can't tell you how provoked I am! The idea!"

"Here's a thought: my old English/German German/English dictionary is in the bookcase in Amidships. Put that on the breakfast table and both of you can work off it. And of course I'll talk to them—put them on the phone."

About ten minutes later, the husband was beaming. Apparently, Charlie had answered a number of questions he hadn't been able to ask me. And when I plunked the huge Langenscheidts dictionary down on the breakfast table, all was forgiven. On Friday, the husband consulted the dictionary, then said to me, "I think maybe you are liking ancient music?" He had heard me playing some Renaissance stuff.

"Ja, ja," I replied eagerly. He responded by giving me one of the finest "ancient" CDs now in my collection: a double set featuring some gorgeous medieval German chants. Better than MoH deserved (given the antics of bad Charlie). I tried to make it up to them by giving them lots of breakfast in the morning and lots of strong drink in the afternoon.

# CHAPTER 12

The summer of MoH's second season continued busy, with three or four rooms booked many nights running. I had turned the corner: the money was pouring in. When I did the laundry, I found checks stuffed into my jeans pockets and cash jammed into my aprons. (This is an occupational hazard: people give you what they owe you wherever you happen to be, and you thank them and put it away rather than rushing to the cashbox, which looks grasping. I'm still finding payments from who knows whom or when.)

Toby pretty much stayed in Barnstable. I guess I couldn't blame him. He called every single night, and our conversations warmed my heart. He was affectionate, thoughtful, funny—all the good stuff. I continued to adore him. When he came once in June on a Wednesday and Thursday that I had no guests, we drove to the school where he'd taught. It was a glorious day, and we walked around the campus hand in hand. He proudly showed me the window of the place where he'd first lived with his wife and two toddlers. To my horror, it was a basement window with a well. As much as I loved him, I could never have lived like that.

Each week that summer the procession of guests continued to increase. Toby also came for a visit over the Fourth of July weekend, but the intense level of activity in the house bothered him. At least I'd refurbished the bedroom where we usually stayed. As an insomniac, he would have deeply disliked the bunk beds and the voyeuristic fish. I didn't blame him for not coming often. I was crazy busy and probably not much fun to talk to, so obsessed was I with taking care of the guests. The last thing a significant other wants to hear is that you spent the afternoon making muffins that didn't rise, which you think was because the baking powder had gotten old, so you'll have to do the whole thing all over again…and so forth. I really wasn't thinking much about him. I was just so busy.

It was at that point that I decided not to accept any more one-night rentals, at least during the busy summer and fall seasons. The one-nighters are lucrative, because they're numerous—people always want to come for a night, especially if they are on their way someplace else—but it's much more work. It requires a lot of bed-changing and bathroom cleaning, not to mention load after load of laundry every couple of days. I feared for those Maytag top-of-the-line-ten-years-ago Neptune machines.

I had actually tried a laundry service the first year, but it had proved unsatisfactory: my lovely linen napkins and elegant old cotton pillowcases came back rough-dried and rumpled. And a pillowcase with my grand-mother's monogram embroidered on it in blue was destroyed completely (my fault: I shouldn't have sent it). If I was going to have to iron them, I might as well wash them. I realize I could have bought polyester and skipped the ironing stage altogether, but I was determined to use what I had: I also thought it was more elegant. (My dining room has mauve strié wallpaper and a huge old ormolu and gold chandelier, which calls for an intense response.) And there was a disappointing experience with some towels that came back with huge bleach stains. The service seemed deeply uninterested in replacing them. So, back to multiple loads of laundry every couple of days. Nobody had warned me about the trials of laundry. I prob-ably wouldn't have listened.

Even with the two-night minimum, I felt tired to the bone. That ex-pression about being asleep before your head hits the pillow pretty much describes my good-night arc. Once when I visited Toby in Barnstable, I was so tired that all I did was lie in a chair on the porch and watch the birds. I felt like an 80-year-old.

People always asked, "Why don't you hire a teenage girl from the neighborhood to make those beds and help you with the housework, muf-fins, beds, etc.?" The answer is twofold. First, I was, as I've mentioned, mar-ried to the concept of the money. I was paying a large quarterly property tax, and I paid Ben, whose good works kept the house from leaking, catch-ing fire, or falling down. To clear the money I needed, I had to maximize my profits by minimizing my overhead. Second, though they say teenagers want work and have a hard time finding it, this is not true everywhere. That teenage girl either doesn't exist anywhere near me, or she's playing tennis on the national circuit or crewing on a windjammer in Greece.

Connie took exception to my precision bathroom cleaning one day when I was whining on the phone.

"You never crawl around like that before I come to visit."

"That's because you know you're dealing with friendly germs—my friends' germs, or mine. The guests at the B & B have no idea whose germs they're dealing with. It's creepy to find a stranger's hair or toothpaste on the bathroom floor, and the only way I can be sure to get rid of it all is to crawl around, as you put it."

"Well, don't complain to me if you're tired. It sounds as if you're into overkill, or outright martyrdom."

A pleasant couple from California visited for a few days. They asked about my husband when they heard I was a widow and I told them he'd been 80 when he died. They mentioned their daughter was a recent widow who'd also married a much older man. She lived on a horse farm with 24 beautiful Andalusians.

I guess my face must have registered "Wow!" I don't hang out with too many people who have dozens of horses.

"Actually," said the wife, "She was married to Tony Curtis."

"Omigosh! Tony Curtis was your son-in-law!"

"Yes," said her husband. "And he was a year older than I am."

Just three degrees of separation from Tony Curtis! A tiny brush with celebrity.

I took a weekend off in midsummer without guests. Toby and I were invited to my friend's hunting and fishing camp in the Adirondacks for a long weekend. It was a large house party, and somehow, when they weren't winded from hiking, tennis, or climbing mountains, the eight or ten other women in the group decided they were going to participate in our wedding. The thought of these 70-somethings as bridesmaids struck them and the rest of us as pretty funny—Toby and I and our supposed wedding provided amusement throughout the weekend, Toby playing along cheerfully.

Apparently I had bragged to our host and hostess that Toby was a super cook, and a day before we left, they suggested that Toby should fix omelets out of the refrigerator leftovers. I thought that was a difficult assignment—18 omelets out of nothing? For people he'd known for two days?—and I admired Toby very much for simply agreeing, then turning to the task. As my mother used to say, if they ask you to sing or play the guitar, do it. Do it right away, without saying you couldn't possibly: eventually you're going to have to because they won't give up until you do. Note that he also had some terrible equipment to work with: skillets from maybe the '50s (nothing nonstick) and a very floppy metal spatula. But the result was spectacular.

We had omelets made of grilled vegetables; we had omelets made of ham, and olives and green peppers and salmon. We had omelets made with *smoked* salmon with onions and capers; omelets made with various cheeses. Toby was creative with the herbs, and the omelets were so good we shared them all. I was really proud of him.

On the way home, we listened to the music on our respective iPods and were amazed at how many pieces were beloved by both of us, from Schubert's "Trout Quintet" to "The Lion Sleeps Tonight" by the Tokens.

Back to work. A woman came up from the Cape to see her lawyer in Salem. She was about my age and said she was divorcing her second husband, which was the reason for the visit. I'm thinking maybe Husband Number Three was in the wings: she wandered around the house with her cell phone talking intensely to someone.

Somehow we got on the subject of her first husband. She had divorced him as well, because he was a serious drug user. He had died not too long afterwards of a combination of cocaine and heroin.

"It was a terrible shame: he was a brilliant actor—he did comedy roles in the movies. He did a late-night TV show too. And he could sing: he did a lot of records. And the whole time he was doing drugs practically non-stop." She sighed.

"I was still in love with him: I think I still am, a little. I just couldn't take the lifestyle."

"I'm so sorry."

"He was only 33 when he died."

Suddenly, as the Brits say, the penny dropped. The Cape. The drugs. The movies and the music. Dead at 33. I said, "You weren't married to—" I said, mentioning an actor whose name in the '80s was a household word.

"Yeah," she answered.

OMG. I was amazed. And utterly thrilled to have this woman in my house! Talk about a brush with stardom.

When Toby called that night, I couldn't wait to tell him. He was un-impressed.

"I feel like a celebrity," I said.

"You're not a celebrity, sweetie. *She's* not even a celebrity. And that was a sad life."

"Well, okay, you're right, of course. The whole thing was sad. And I feel for her. But isn't it just a little bit magical to have her here?"

"If you say so," he laughed.

"If you come up, you can meet her."

"What are you thinking?? That is so not going to happen. All those people walking around your house and we're hiding in the kitchen. Plus, I get no pleasure out of watching you work your charming you-know-what off."

"You could help."

"I had a job for forty years. I'm retired now. But thanks for the offer. Love you."

The famous actor's ex-wife vanished out of my life two days later. But when I changed her bed, I found a very cute little Banana Republic t-shirt. I called to let her know. She said it wasn't hers. But who else's could it have been? Now I own the t-shirt of the ex-wife of a big star. Now that really is celebrity! Or as close to it as I'm likely to get.

My birthday is in July, and my children gave me a real iPhone, my first. I'd been happily using a flippy phone for years, but it wouldn't do email, let alone texting. With the new phone, I could be in Barnstable or just in downtown Marblehead, get an email requesting a room, and respond to the would-be guest immediately. (Timing is important in the B & B business: if you don't get back to them quickly, people tend to move on down the list.) A whole new world!

August came, and with it another flood of interesting guests. I read the fine things the visitors wrote in my beautiful guest book, and I'm afraid I began to believe my own PR. This is how to run a B & B, I thought. I was getting pretty good at this!

Then Barbara arrived.

She seemed nice. She had rented my best room, Starboard Home, for four nights. After staying a night, then another, the next morning she told me she was leaving because the house was awful and the service worse. I was horrified. What on earth had I done, or left undone? No one had ever voiced a complaint (I didn't say this). I refunded the money for the unused nights and begged her to tell me what was wrong. She simply made a grumpy face and took off.

Two days later I got a message from Charlie. "A little bad news, Mumz. Have you seen the review on Trip Advisor?"

In fear and trembling, I took a look. Barbara had outdone herself. Marblehead on Harbor, she reported, had a nice enough view (nice enough!), but there was nothing else to recommend it. She believed the person in charge simply had no idea how to run a B & B. First of all, she noted, the place was "a dump." I'm quoting. The furniture was old and shabby, and the rugs were threadbare. Breakfast was all right, but nothing special. Worst of all, her bed was not made up each day with fresh sheets.

Fresh sheets? Each day? The woman had to be crazy. I objected to her take on my antique rugs and furniture as well. And I truly believed the breakfasts were way above average: Fresh fruit compote and fresh-baked breads every morning? Sausage and cheese strata? There's a woman in Marblehead who leaves her guests a mini-refrigerator with milk and juice and a big box of cereal. Now *that's* a sub-par breakfast. What was wrong with Barbara? What was wrong with me? I sat there brooding and getting teary. Charlie called again, sympathizing with my heartache but giving his opinion that she'd probably shot herself in the foot with the sheets thing.

"I suppose so, but I feel just awful."

"I hear you, Mumzi, and I'm so sorry it happened. But you probably need to develop a thicker skin. You're going to get people who don't like you, your breakfasts, your stairs, your stuff. Don't let it get to you too badly. The main reason I called back is that I forgot to tell you, you have the chance to answer her complaints on Trip Advisor."

Answer her complaints? Revenge! I immediately dashed off a message declaring that one person's shabby carpet was another person's antique Heriz, and that the writer would surely feel more at home in a Motel 6 where everything was new and shiny. And mass-produced.

Then I deleted it and wrote a humble response saying simply how sorry I was that we'd failed to live up to her expectations and hoping that she'd someday give us a chance to show her a better time. Ha. I hoped I'd never lay eyes on her again.

I didn't. But she had an effect on me at a pretty deep level. It was as if I had somehow lost my innocence, simply because *somebody*—albeit only one somebody, and arguably a crackpot at that—didn't approve of the way I was running my business. I seemed to internalize Barbara, and although I still enjoyed running Marblehead on Harbor, I admit that it was never quite the same again. Like a favorite cup broken and, though skillfully mended, never quite the same.

November came, and MoH closed for the winter. Again I enjoyed the luxury of walking around my house barefoot, leaving piles of books in the living room, and generally not hiding in the back of the house. I built fires and curled up with my reading when I wasn't counting how much money I'd made my second season. And I pined for Toby.

# CHAPTER 13

In January, when no one was volunteering to visit Marblehead on Harbor except the lady who enjoyed her annual weekend escape from her mother, Toby came for a month. It was his idea, and I was thrilled.

We didn't do a whole lot during that time, just tucked ourselves in and enjoyed good food, wine, and one another's company. Little by little I learned more about Toby's background. Until his wife's death and his move to Barnstable full-time (they'd spent summers there), he'd been in boarding school all his life. Seriously: his whole life.

True story, amazing as it seems. He was born in a boarding school in New Hampshire, where his father was teaching. They moved to another in Delaware, where his father was headmaster and Toby spent several years. He went off to board at a school in Massachusetts when he was 12.

"Twelve!" I expostulated. "It sounds like the English upper class! Those poor little kids, shipped off at age seven. Weren't you homesick? Didn't you cry?"

"No: it was wonderful. I loved it. It was like being at camp."

He described their sleeping arrangements: there were long rows of cubicles with curtains between the boys' beds. Curtains? I didn't want to know any more.

Toby went from that school to college in Connecticut, graduated, and got a Master's in Education there. He worked and lived in at a school in Connecticut, at his father's school in Delaware, and finally at the boarding school in Massachusetts where he taught French and coached crew until his retirement. I could hardly believe it.

"You and your wife and children all lived at the school?" I thought again how ill-suited I would have been to that life. He nodded. "You've really always lived in a boarding school?" Another nod. And these were almost entirely boys' schools?"

"Affirmative."

"Well, I must say you seem to be doing a remarkable job of living on the outside."

He laughed. "It does catch me unprepared sometimes. I have to mow the grass myself; I even have to change my own light bulbs and wash my own car. Living at a boarding school, we never had to do any of that."

As it became time for the guests to begin arriving, Toby packed up and went back to Barnstable. It was obvious he didn't want to stick around. I missed him, but there was a fair bit of work to do to get ready for my third full season.

An English family arrived—husband and wife with a lovely, well-mannered teenaged daughter. Both the wife and the daughter were open and chatty. They praised the view, the food, the porch, the jigsaw puzzle of New England on the desk in the living room. The husband sat on the porch and read the New York Times online.

Any attempt at conversation when I met the gentleman failed completely. He gave no evidence of appreciating the breakfast, the view, the gentle breeze, etc. I kept trying to figure out what was wrong, but I couldn't read him. Maybe the bed wasn't to his liking?

"Is there anything I can do to make your husband more comfortable?" I asked June.

"Oh, no," she answered. "Everything is ducky!" Except your husband hates the place, I thought darkly.

The day they were due to leave, I tiptoed past him on my way to untangle the flag. He looked up from his laptop.

"Becky," he said. I stopped in my tracks. He knew my name!

"I want you to know this is one of the nicest, most beautiful places I have ever stayed. I'm the CEO of M_____ in Africa, and I've been all over the world.

"I love this house. I love the view. I love the way you run your outfit. I am going to put the best review you've ever gotten on Trip Advisor."

Well, chase my Aunt Fannie up a gum tree. For one of the few times in my life, I was speechless. And he was as good as his word.

Toby continued to email and phone. Because of the (somewhat controlled) chaos in my house once the B & B was open for business, he didn't visit often. This was a problem, because I couldn't leave the B & B when I had guests, which was most of the time. And I wanted to be with him. I realized how much I cared for him: I needed to find a way for us to spend more time together. There had to be people who babysat for B & B owners. I called Ruth to ask whom she used when they went away. She gave me a name, but by the time she'd finished describing him and his way with the guests, not to mention the bar closet, I'd decided to look elsewhere. I called my friend Ann, who knows stuff. "You should talk to Barb," she said. "You'll love her. She and her husband are putting two kids through college, so she'd like the money. And she is very, very competent." Coming from Ann, who practically invented competence, this was high praise.

It was all true. I was crazy about Barb from the get-go. Tall and rangy, with straight dark hair, bangs, and no-nonsense eyeglasses, she breezed in and immediately took control: she seemed to have an instinct for knowing instantly where I kept everything, from the sheets and towels to the pancake turner. We arranged for me to visit Toby over two weekdays when there was just one couple staying at MoH. Afterwards, *both* halves of the couple emailed to say how marvelous Barb was. I hated paying the money, but I knew I needed the breaks, she needed her kids' tuition money, and Toby and I needed time together.

Barb was marvelously proactive: one afternoon, after she'd gotten well into the work, she had two rollaway beds from Jordan's Furniture delivered. "Twenty dollars a night to add a person to any room," she ordained firmly. They paid for themselves in no time. And she persuaded me to buy a king-sized mattress pad and a sort of yoke that turned the twin beds in Amidships into a king bed. Why hadn't I thought of that? There were always more couples who wanted to share a bed than twin-bed sleepers. She found a super bargain on Splenda tastes-like-sugar packets—I'm still working away on the thousand or so she bought, but it really was a bargain. She could also make a bed so tight you could use it for a trampoline. She knew how to fold a contour sheet flat. This is a secret only four people in the world know. And when she washed the wine glasses, there was never, ever a spot.

From the moment she walked in the door, Barb was a part of Marblehead on Harbor, and an invaluable help. I could now take a suitcase and run down to Barnstable to be with Toby, knowing that all the guests would love her. Things were looking up indeed.

I wrote up a memo for her with all the information I thought she'd need. She could do the whole thing blindfolded on common sense and intuition, but it seemed like the right thing to do. Just to show you how much detail went into every day at Marblehead on Harbor, I've included it as an appendix at the end of the book

# CHAPTER 14

The summer proceeded and MoH was bustling. Then came July. It was a Saturday morning, around 7:00 a.m. I was fixing breakfast for six guests when I heard some very serious machinery close by. I opened the door and saw that the millionaire across the street was reengineering his landscape, surely waking my guests in the process. Saturday morning? Come on.

This otherwise charming millionaire (actually multi-) and his wife had recently erected a three-car garage adjoining their house, the second house down the beach from me, with an indoor swimming pool that has a really gorgeous glass roof. It gives the impression of an elegant 19$^{th}$ century conservatory or greenhouse. He had run into problems with the town Zoning Board, which pointed out that he didn't have enough side setback to put up this addition. Fazed not at all by this crimp in his plans, he bought the house next door to him, the very first one along the beach, which gave him the footage he needed. You can do this when you are worth many millions! That house, a very pretty copy of a Federal-era mansion painted a tasteful yellow with white woodwork and dark shutters, proceeded to sit there, pretty much vacant. Somebody said he used it as an office. (I joked that he should let me add it to Marblehead on Harbor: I remembered it had at least eight bedrooms, probably each with its own bath.)

Now bulldozers, or front-end loaders or whatever you call them, were ripping up the driveway to the first house, just across from me. Sometimes the vehicles would stop and several people would begin jack-hammering. The din was fearful. I quickly organized breakfast, realizing that my crew would be coming down early: no one could sleep through this.

I apologized to everyone for the noise and explained that I had had no warning about this. In fact, I didn't even know just what was happening. The group took it well, saying they hadn't planned to eat on the porch anyway (people often took food out and sat contemplating the boats and beach).

After breakfast was over, but not the awful noise, I ran over to my neighbor up the street, who was on the Zoning Board, to ask him what our gazillionaire was planning. David explained that he was ripping up his driveway.

"I get that," I told him. "But why? It's in good shape."

"He's going to make the two driveways into one, to unify the properties. There'll be just one driveway making a big wiggly half-circle with parking on the edges and all made of the same type of stone—pavers. I think it's going to look nice. And then he's going to re-landscape the whole thing."

Uh oh. How long was this going to take? I went back to the house with a heavy heart: my guests were going to suffer. Who wants to sit on the porch with backhoes roaring and beeping and dust flying?

This continued for most of the day. Happily, most of the time most of the guests were touring Marblehead, getting lunch, and shopping. By 4:00 p.m. everybody was back taking showers to get ready for their evenings. The Philbricks were going to a wedding; Ilana and Jane were heading out for dinner with two match.com dates (!); Joyce and Jack were visiting their son and his wife in Cambridge; and I was off to the movies with four friends. The hot water held out. The electricity did not. Apparently, when four hairdryers are on, it quits. I heard cries from the third floor bedroom! The second-floor bathroom! Starboard Home! And my hair dryer lay dead in my hands, as did, judging from the reactions, everyone else's.

"Okay, everybody, stay calm," I hollered up the stairs. "Just sit there without your appliances—do your makeup or something—and try to be patient while I fix the problem."

Ha. I hadn't a lot of confidence I *could* fix it. Unfortunately, there was no one else.

I have mentioned that my late husband Larry was dynamite on all household issues—he could repair the disposal, wire the new CD player to play through the old speakers, and so on. Needless to say, since I hadn't had to, I had no relationships with repair people and I myself had learned almost nothing. I was completely unprepared.

I had to stop and remind myself that we don't have fuses anymore: we have something called circuit breakers, and they are in the basement where the fuse box used to be. I took a flashlight and went down into the bowels of the basement, which has almost no natural light and has become a lair for people who hoard. I pretty much hate it. I opened the box and turned all the switches the wrong way. This effectively shut off my computer and all the electronic clocks. Unfortunately, nothing else happened. I stood there, thinking it might be a good time to run away. I felt immediately ashamed: was that any way to run a B & B? But I was frightened: my hands were actually shaking. I thought how angry they would all be with me if I couldn't get the electricity going quickly. Shades of Barbara the awful guest thronged into my mind, eroding my confidence in my ability to deal with the problem.

I went back up the stairs, thinking. In the computer room, I recollected seeing a small gray box low on the wall inside a cupboard. It had a cover similar to the cover on the big circuit breaker box. Maybe, just maybe, there were circuit breakers in that box also. So I wedged most of myself into the cupboard, opened the box and there, in Larry's meticulous, tiny printing, was a switch that said, "3rd floor." I couldn't decipher the other glyphs, but I was praying they were for bathrooms and bedrooms as well. I spared a thought for how wonderful Larry had been. And wished I could tell him so. The careful, familiar handwriting made me want to weep.

Before I switched anything, I knocked on all the doors and asked each of the ladies when she had to be ready: we agreed on a staggered arrangement that I hoped wouldn't put such a strain on the power. Then I thwacked away at the switches, which were horribly hard to budge, especially given that I was unsteadily squatting in a two-foot high cupboard and trying to manipulate switches on the left-hand wall about seven inches from the ground. I finished; I switched them back on. My hands were now bleeding. But I heard joyful noises from the bathrooms and realized we had ignition and liftoff. My movie, luckily, wasn't till 7:30, so I waited till all of them had set out, then did my own hair. Having a little extra time, I also reset all the clocks, no mean feat.

So you could say all's well that ends well, I guess. Actually, these are the times that try a hostess's soul. And make you long for a partner to share the fun. Ironically, if Larry hadn't been ill, I truly think he would have loved to run the B & B with me. He loved people, he loved to feed them and give them drinks, he loved fixing things, and he would've adored the money.

As I mentioned, the best and longest-running B &Bs seemed to be run by a couple, or sisters. What a shame Toby had negatory interest in Marblehead on Harbor.

We'd spoken over the summer about managing the distance between us. To me it felt almost like being in college and having a boyfriend at a college hours away. I suggested we could try living in one house for six months, the other for the other six.

"Maybe not *six* months," Toby said. I figured he wanted more months in his house. Hmm. We'd see about that.

But it could have been worse: I wonder what it would've been like to run MoH if I'd been alone. I mean, *really* alone. I had my ups and downs. But I had my two children not just nearby, but almost always supportive and helpful. I had wonderful friends at a distance who kept in touch, and friends in Marblehead who included me in dinners out and outings. And a very nice man, who'd always been a friend of Larry's and continued respectful and kind to him up to the end, offered to marry me if I wanted company! And I had Toby. You could say I sometimes felt alone, but never abandoned.

Back to our millionaire and his noise: there were days that were good and days that were bad. I took to telling potential guests there was an issue of noise from the house across the street, so that they could back out. I don't recall anyone having a change of heart after hearing this. Good sports, my guests.

But the best was yet to come. By the end of the season, not only was the driveway reconfigured, but a multitude of amazing trees, shrubbery, and flowers began to appear. My neighbor had had the entire property landscaped with lilacs, lilies, masses of purple cranesbill geraniums, a huge crimson trumpet vine embracing a side porch pillar, and hydrangeas of all kinds: blue, white lacecap, and pink paniculata; weeping cedar, cypress, arborvitae standing at attention; and lovely new bright green sod. From being a noisy eyesore, the property had become a resounding enhancement to Marblehead on Harbor. I was grateful, and glad I hadn't fussed, and I wrote him a note saying how much I loved the new look.

I then took a look at what *he* had to look at: my garden at MoH was mostly for cutting flowers for the public rooms and little nosegays for the bedrooms. It had just sort of grown up over the years, with day lilies, baptisia, and peonies, with huge puffy white Annabelle hydrangeas in the back: these are terrific for cutting to put in the public rooms. And my two stands of pink phlox were lovely, except that when you cut phlox, it drops its flowers after about a day. As for the lawn, it was a disaster. It always was, by midsummer, and I hesitated to water: Marblehead is always asking us to conserve water. So there it sat, brown, ugly, and crackly as Rice Krispies.

I was greatly comforted when a guest who worked in environmental studies told me, "When I see a green lawn by the ocean, I get suspicious."

I was nonetheless thrilled to look over and see the millionaire's beautiful green lawn with its wonderful plantings. And I hoped he cast his eyes on *his* property and not on mine.

# CHAPTER 15

The profusion of guests was a two- edged sword: Though I was delighted to have the business, it also meant a certain amount of confusion for me. I was learning that I don't handle a too-full agenda very well: at the same time, the money continued to fascinate me. I was still getting bills and notices about various types of money we owed, so I continued to feel anxious and consequently took on more than perhaps I should have. I was also still strongly dedicated to saving wherever possible.

I had been so badly frightened by the void Larry's behavior (though not his fault) had left in our finances that I economized every way I could. Market Basket turned out to have not only cheap paper goods, but downright excellent quiches. This was great news for me: if you can buy inexpensive tomato and spinach, ham and cheese, and asparagus quiches, etc., why would you bake them? The place even has good produce, though you have to pick and choose carefully, and I was able to get lovely blueberries, raspberries, melons, and grapes to construct fruit compotes that were much admired at breakfast. English muffins, ham, cookies, all were at least 20 percent less than anywhere else.

But wait! There's more! On the Lynnway, about six miles from Marblehead on Harbor, right next door to the Green Tea Chinese restaurant, is a remarkable store called Dollar Tree. It's part of a national chain about fifty years old, and if there's one near you, run, don't walk. I think my house cleaner Diana put me onto this. Do not confuse this store with the Family Dollar, Dollar Store, or any of those other "Dollar" places. Dollar Tree actually sells *every*thing for a dollar! This means a package of shower curtain liners costs a dollar! The boxes of Kleenex cost a dollar! A toilet brush costs a dollar! Picture my delight as I raced through the store, madly snatching up item after item. The first time I shopped there, I didn't really believe the hype: you couldn't make money selling these things for just a dollar, could you? I got to the register with 40 items in my cart; I left after paying exactly $40. I could hardly believe it and was ecstatic. Of course, the house always wins: the store makes money on purchases that would cost *less* than a dollar elsewhere. I didn't care. I shopped carefully and I pretty much knew how much everything cost at the local grocery or CVS. What I needed were the toiletries and amenities I put into the basket in each bathroom—you know, the things people forget to make sure are in their overnight kits, such as toothbrushes, Band-Aids, travel-size deodorant, and so forth. This store was absolutely perfect for my purposes.

I also tried very, very hard not to waste anything. If I was making a strata and had an extra egg yolk or white, in it went. If guests on separate days had eaten half of two quiches, the two halves went into a pie plate together, and voila! Two different kinds of quiche for the incoming guests. Leftover hard-boiled eggs became egg salad for me. I saved and reused everything I could.

I slashed my personal budget across the board. I stopped shopping for clothes, except for an occasional foray into a promising thrift shop. For lunch I ate whatever the guests had left on the sideboard, and my diet at dinner often featured fruit compote, peanut butter on banana bread, and eggs. I pretty much stopped entertaining, which saved a lot of money, and none of my friends were offended, as my schedule obviously didn't admit many evenings when the dining room was unquestionably mine. I got my hair cut at Silver Shears, the barbershop frequented by the men and children of Marblehead (Walk-Ins Welcome!). I quit having manicures (not that I'd indulged often). I used my late mother's old lipsticks. My books came from the library instead of Amazon.com, and I watched Turner Classic Movies on TV. An occasional movie and dinner out with the girls (the pool of single women in town features both charm and brains) was a treat to which I looked forward a lot.

I made mistakes, of course. Occasionally, the cream was found to have gone west, or south, or wherever cream goes when it's undrinkable. The guests were good sports about this, but they'd have to start over with a new bowl of cereal or cup of coffee, so it was a bother for them and actually not a good way to save money. I also ordered the New York Times and Boston

Globe for the guests. I noticed they often appeared unread, and eventually noticed that most of the guests got their news online. Realizing this, I canceled both papers. Fortunately, neither cream nor newspapers represented a large outlay.

One morning I decided to reheat a hardboiled egg, left over from the guests' breakfast the day before, in the microwave. It was cold from the refrigerator, so I gave it a good minute. I cracked off the shell and took a bite.

Have you ever had an airbag go off next to your ear? This is the sensation I experienced as the egg blew up—actually blew up in pieces—in my face with a loud retort. I wound up with a blistered lip and a bright red chin. In an effort to garner sympathy, I made the mistake of mentioning this episode to my family over dinner at Sarah's. After they had stopped screaming with laughter, they got so involved in the physics of the egg, the heat, the probability that a small drop of uncooked yolk in the center of the egg had caused the explosion, that my pain and suffering were forgotten altogether. But the burn took a week to go away. After that I ate my eggs cold. Again, expenditure was minimal.

One very important money-saver was not of my devising but is an automatic and desirable perk of running a bed and breakfast. You can legitimately deduct a healthy percentage of many, many things you buy or consume for the B & B. This includes, for example, part of the cost of plants you put in the garden and the flowers you buy for the house, the cost of the breakfast foods your guests eat and the bottles of water they drink; even a percentage of heat and AC—water—your sewerage bill. It's incredibly gratifying. This is all blessed by my tax advisor, because it's true.

Habitual miserliness across the board increased my take and my sense of self-worth. I felt good about saving money, and I felt capable. Although it's obvious I didn't have a lot of life, at least not during B & B season, I was managing to make up for a lot of the money we'd lost, so I also felt more confident, less afraid, about my finances. The wolf wasn't coming to my door again if I could help it.

Some people are so appealing and authentic you warm to them immediately and, if you run a B & B, wish they'd stay and live with you. The Cohus, down from Quebec, were just that kind, and I was delighted they were making a week's stay. Arthur was gray-haired with a serious mustache, Michele a vibrant and zaftig brunette. Michele adored the beach and was down the steps hunting sea glass at least once a day

"Where did you get the pink and green stained-glass window in the downstairs bathroom?" Arthur asked me one morning.

"I bought it on the South Shore from an outfit that used to sell detail from old houses," I answered. "It was a birthday present for Larry when we'd been married just a few years."

"It's a lovely window," he noted. "But do you realize how dirty it is?"

"It is? How embarrassing! I never thought about it."

"Do you have any car polish?"

"Does the Pope wear a dress? Larry collected cars and did a lot of work on them himself. I probably have a gallon down in the garage."

Arthur took car polish and a soft rag, and within an hour my window gleamed as never before. The Cohus were my only guests that week: we drank wine on the porch if the weather was warm enough, and in the living room if it wasn't. Michele had a birthday, and I gave her a bottle of Sea Glass sauvignon blanc and a card with sea glass on the front. I felt like crying when they left—the pain only somewhat mitigated by the inch-high wad of American currency Arthur pressed into my hand.

Toby called to ask me whether I had an afternoon without guests in the next week or two to have some visitors for lunch.

"Fairly special visitors, in fact," he said.

"There's nobody around next Wednesday: my only guests are leaving promptly that morning because they have a plane to catch. Who is it?"

"It's Sarah and George," he said, naming his daughter and her husband. "They've been really eager to pay you a visit, check out the house, see where I have all this fun, et cetera."

"Oh, that's wonderful! I haven't seen Charlie for weeks." Charlie was their two-year-old.

"Not so fast." Toby said they'd gotten a sitter for Charlie because they wanted to be able to focus on us rather than Charlie—which was a good idea, though I loved seeing him. A two-year-old tends to suck up all the attention in the room. And they were paying a sitter to come visit me!

I was delighted. I fixed a shrimp salad plate with deviled eggs and fresh tomatoes and made a pitcher of iced tea. It was a lovely mild day, and we had lunch on the porch, made comments on the boats, and enjoyed each other's company. I felt special, like someone important to their family.

One Sunday afternoon late in the summer Toby and I went out with my close friends Ann and Dudley on their boat. We had a beautiful afternoon and were drinking lightly and puttering around the harbor, there being very little wind. We decided to head out of the harbor and look for some. Before we left the harbor, I checked my home phone via cell phone, just to make sure I didn't need to respond to a guest request, and received a nasty shock: "This is Catherine Putnam, just calling to confirm that my friend Peg and I plan to arrive at about three o'clock. We look forward to meeting you and enjoying your lovely home."

I looked at my watch. It was 3:20. My stomach tumbled into the nether regions.

"Oh, my God!" I expostulated. "I forgot a guest! I have to go home— I'm so sorry, but I have to leave. I'm afraid she's already arrived. This is awful!" I realized I was blithering. Fortunately, Ann and Dudley are rarely if ever thrown by *any*thing, and this didn't even slow them down. Dudley motored gently up to the Corinthian Yacht Club dock, about 200 yards from my house, and I jumped off. Toby not being a spry sort, and presumably having a nice time and in no way responsible for the mess I was in, stayed aboard with the Welches. His car was at the Boston Yacht Club dock, where they'd be returning.

I raced up the dock, across the parking lot and down the lane to Marblehead on Harbor. A car sat in the driveway, looking, I thought, vaguely reproachful. I tore up the steps and saw two ladies gently rocking on the porch, looking at the harbor. I wondered if they had seen the mad dash and realized who it must be. Out of breath and gasping, I introduced myself and burst into a litany of apologies.

"It's really all right," said Catherine. "We're honestly just enjoying the view." But she sounded a little frosty, and who could blame her?

"I hope you came in and found your room. I'm so terribly sorry. For some reason I had you down as coming in later." This wasn't entirely true, but it seemed better than saying I just forgot all about you.

"No. We said three o'clock, I'm sure." I deserved that.

"Let me show you around a bit, give you the tour you should've started with." Fortunately the room hadn't been used earlier that weekend and was all ready to go. I made sure they knew which was their bathroom and reminded them of the vagaries of early 20$^\text{th}$-century plumbing. I showed them over the dining room, with its guest refrigerator and coffee/tea machine. I told them the breakfast hours (7:30—9:30) and noted that the living room and porch were for the guests' exclusive use. I gave them the notebook of local menus—all interspersed with abject apologies. I couldn't seem to stop. I realized that they had begun to feel sorry for me and I hated myself: it was unconscious, but it was a sort of manipulation—a manipulation from a position of weakness, unworthy in the extreme.

While they settled into their room, I uncorked a bottle of extra-good

Chardonnay, stuck it in my silver ice bucket, grabbed two glasses and plunked it all down in front of their door. My final appeasement offering.

Catherine and Peg seemed delighted with the Chardonnay and went off to Salem for dinner. Toby arrived a few minutes after, pleased at having had a bit of sailing after all. It was so fortunate we hadn't been too far out at sea when I made my discovery. We settled down to drinks and dinner in the kitchen, and I tried to put the afternoon behind me. After all, it was good to be with Toby. But the draggy feeling in my stomach didn't really go away until the ladies did, and even then I felt unhappy and off balance. Once again I asked myself: Was I too disorganized to run a bed and breakfast? Why had another glitch occurred? Was I losing it? None of my systems had worked in today's debacle: my index cards, my notebook, my notes to myself everywhere—all had failed me. Or I had failed them. My self-esteem plunged. Keeping the house up seemed to be tearing my confidence down.

October brought the usual suspects—witches, warlocks, the Scream, and so forth. My little witches were back for Hallowe'en, along with a number of other guests. And Marblehead on Harbor closed out its third season.

# CHAPTER 16

Toby came again for a long month in January and the beginning of February. I was overjoyed. At Christmas, he'd presented me with a card inviting me to fly to Paris with him in the spring (we would share other expenses). This was also very exciting. I had been there in the summer of 1967, the year I graduated from college, so it had been a while. How perfect to see this romantic city again, and with someone I loved.

My fourth full season looked as if it would be incredibly busy. I'd been booking guests since February: word about Marblehead on Harbor had gotten around. It was exciting, but it scared me. The busier I got, the more I feared making mistakes.

I was amazed that the terrible review on Trip Advisor apparently hadn't slowed my customers down. I guess people can spot an outlier, and that woman was as far out as you can get. Fresh sheets on the bed daily? That isn't even earth friendly. And yet her off-base putdown had reached deep inside me. As Charlie had said, there would always be people who didn't like my stairs, my mattresses, my food, and/or me. It's just something you have to deal with. So develop a thicker skin? Easier said than done. New things scare me: witness my sheer terror at the prospect of my first guest, Rita the Terrible. From the moment of Barbara's review, the B & B had changed subtly for me—became something potentially unfriendly, maybe even dangerous. I kept at it, but when guests left saying or writing that they'd had a wonderful time, I breathed a sigh of relief—another hurdle cleared. I was feeling the downside risk of the enterprise more than the pleasure of accomplishment.

I had corralled Barb to run the B & B for my week in April with Toby.

"I bet he'll propose to you in Paris!" she exclaimed. "How incredibly romantic!" That sounded terrific to me, though I wasn't holding my breath. I hadn't heard any marriage talk lately.

Early in April, off we flew. Toby had found an apartment to rent in a lovely old building on the Ile de la Cité. It looked fantastic. I couldn't wait. I could hardly believe it when we arrived, very late at night for us, early in the morning for them. We had trouble getting our key but managed to raise our landlady and flop down, exhausted. When we woke, it was late afternoon. We had slept away the best part of the day! I took a good look at our lodgings; we were in a loft bedroom, and it was hard to sit up because the ceiling was so close. Edgar Allan Poe would have been sure he'd been buried alive. I had to crawl over Toby each night to get to my side of the bed: he said it was an extremely sexy experience. The stuff in my suitcase, since I couldn't open it more than halfway, quickly got sort of stirred around and balled up. But that afternoon I put on my skinny jeans and out we went.

We strolled a little, then went grocery shopping. We put money into a kitty and Toby bought a lot, really a lot of stuff. I wasn't exactly sure why. We saw the inside of the Sainte-Chapelle with the afternoon sun pouring through the red and blue stained glass. It was so gorgeous it could make a believer out of anyone. We saw the outside of Notre Dame, as there was a set of bleachers set up for some fête or other. We met a nice young man who told us the entire history of Notre Dame, which of course we'd forgotten. I took some beautiful pictures. But we got into the line for the very top of the cathedral by mistake, so we never saw the interior (Toby couldn't have walked all the way up.) He'd mentioned going to Saint Somebody or Other each Sunday to hear the organist play, and I'd hoped we could go and listen, but it never happened. We never went to a concert either. But I didn't care too much: I mostly wanted to be with him.

I soon found out why all the food shopping. We had breakfast in the apartment: croissants with apricot jam and some pretty good coffee. For lunch we went back to the apartment also, except for one day when we split a Croque Monsieur from a street vendor. Half of one sandwich. And one afternoon we sat on the Champs Elysées and had a glass of wine. We ate dinner in the apartment almost every night, except for the night we took a bottle of wine and some bread and cheese to the end of the island and drank it with many hugs and kisses. It was only one night — our very last night before departure — that we went out for dinner. I was puzzled: I knew Toby watched his pennies carefully, but isn't Paris the place you save your pennies *for*? At least gastronomically. Again, it was whatever Toby wanted, and I said nothing, finally deciding he was recreating his student days, when he really was more or less penniless.

Speaking of which, we were on the Metro on our way to the Louvre when Toby lost his wallet—pilfered by someone very skillful. He never felt it. We went through his pockets, hardly able to believe it. We went to the local police station and told our sad tale. Of course nothing came of it: that wallet and our money were gone. He spent a morning canceling his credit cards, which was a good move. A less good move was to get a whole lot more euros. It made no sense.

"Toby," I tried to get through to him. "I have plenty of euros. Let's just use them up, and we can get more later if we need them." It was as though I hadn't spoken—the afternoon was also given up to trying to find a bank that would honor his request immediately. It was almost spooky how unreasonably, at least from my point of view, he was behaving.

Unfortunately, the next day was the Feast of the Assumption of the Virgin, and all the banks were closed. At this point I should have taken a stand and gone to a museum I'd been really eager to visit, the Jacquemart-André. Toby had pooh-poohed their advertised 17th and 18th century paintings, so he wouldn't have minded, and he certainly had his own agenda. But I stayed with him.

With two days left of our trip, he got his darned pile of euros, and sunshine dawned again on the Ile de la Cité. We went to the Musée d'Orsay and saw a lot of Impressionist paintings. We went to the Monet Museum and looked at all those water lilies. For hours. Did I mention I'm not a huge fan of the Impressionists? We saw the Rodin Museum, which was glorious and which we both loved. We never got to the Louvre, though with time running out perhaps it would've been too much to take in. On our last night we went out, as I said, to a very good, though not amazing, restaurant, where for the first time I had more than enough good food to eat and felt I was finally part of the City of Light.

When we landed in Boston, Toby took his many euros to the currency booth and exchanged them for dollars. As we went out the door, he hissed, "Hurry up, Becky! She gave me twice as much as she should have!"

Shame, double shame on me: I was dying to get home before the grandchildren went to bed, and I followed him and said nothing. I felt awful later: I still feel bad. I hope the poor lady didn't lose her job or have to make up the difference. And so home. I felt deflated. I had expected a different experience. But I'd been to Paris with Toby: what was I complaining about?

Back to MoH. Cindy and Rick had come back, to my delight. I still have trouble figuring out how someone whose knee has been immobilized by a steel rod running from calf to thigh can get herself around Marblehead so handily: she even hiked up Castle Rock, a short but steep climb. She is amazing—and so is Rick, clearly crazy about her and subtly helpful. Their visit lifted my spirits.

One Sunday afternoon two weeks after our trip, when Toby had come for the weekend but was leaving the next morning, I felt a little down. I'd been thinking about Paris and how the sort-of-expected proposal hadn't happened, so I decided to talk to Toby about it. Better than letting it eat away at me.

"Toby, we haven't talked about marriage for a long time," I said.

"Well," he answered, "I guess that's because I'm not really in favor of it."

"You used to be—at least the first time I came down to Barnstable you said, 'We could get married.' I remember it very clearly: you said we could get married and I asked where we'd live and you said people often get married first and worry about housing later. Don't you remember?"

"I never said that."

I was taken aback. I knew he *had* said it. You don't forget that kind of thing, especially when you're in the early stages of love. But he'd also been flirting with the idea of our getting married for the past year and a half: "Andy wants to know when I'm going to make an honest woman of you." And that bridesmaid foolishness in the Adirondacks—he'd played along enthusiastically. Once, visiting friends for a weekend, he'd even kissed the bottom of a wine bottle after our hostess had told him this would guarantee you'd be married within the year.

"The fact is, my marriage was so perfect that I can't imagine ever marrying anyone else. I think I'd always be making comparisons." He smiled. I felt like hitting him.

Making comparisons with a woman whose salient feature was her organizational ability? A woman he'd once told me preferred, excuse me, plastic Christmas trees and romance novels? I'd made excuses for her, but seriously. Where was it that I didn't measure up? I hid my hurt and dismay as well as I could.

But that night I gave way to the pain and disappointment, and to the feeling of having been misled. While Toby slept, I cried my eyes out quietly. .How could he? How could he pretend he'd never talked about marriage with me? That he hadn't toyed with the concept again and again? And to add insult to injury, go on to tell me how perfect his marriage had been? When I was cried out, I gave my pillow a thump and fell asleep.

# CHAPTER 17

One midsummer day a woman called to ask if she might come to look at the house: she was planning a wedding and wanted to put up a large family group. Now I had been cautioned by several veterans of the B & B trade not to let wedding parties in. Not ever. Not even if you're broke. Wedding guests, sure. Wedding parties—bridesmaids, groomsmen, and the like, no. The knock on them is that people are often very keyed up—this is especially true of the mother of the bride, for example. And wedding parties tend to drink too much: this means noisy, up late at night, using the plumbing extensively, and possibly destructive of their environment. You know: red wine on the white sofas, cigarette burns on the tables, that sort of thing. I heard and had always obeyed.

But this person was incredibly charming on the phone. I told her to come on over. She arrived promptly, and she was gorgeous as well as charming. She was petite, with a cascade of dark red hair that would have done Lady Godiva proud, lovely green eyes, and the most beautiful white teeth I've ever seen (I have mediocre teeth and am accordingly sensitive to other people's). She'd brought a young girl with her who was, she said, a cousin of her fiancé. So she herself was the bride!

I was fascinated, questioning immediately whether her husband was good enough for her. She told me her name was Melissa, and she and Simon, her intended, lived on the ocean side of Marblehead Neck, about a mile from me. After telling me this, she turned to the cousin and burst into a torrent of rapid, very idiomatic French—explaining what she'd just said to me. I don't speak very good French any more, but I'd been a whiz in high school (I have medals from the French government to prove it) and could pick up what she was saying. Yet her English was totally idiomatic and without any foreign accent.

"Melissa, you're totally bilingual. I'm awed. How did you come by two languages?" I asked.

"It was easy," she laughed. "My mother is French, my father was American."

Color me absolutely won over. I just hoped she would find the house suitable. We looked through all the rooms and decided I could fit them all in. She paused and let out another beautiful ripple of French to the cousin. The cousin didn't actually talk much: probably as stunned by Melissa as I was. And would it be possible to add a few more just for breakfast? Why not? I said. At $10 a person? Bring it on.

When the time came, seven aunts, uncles, and cousins trooped in from Logan Airport. It was Friday and they were all headed for the rehearsal dinner. Much ironing of party clothes ensued, and they all got off on time and in style. I note for the record that they were beautifully behaved when they got back, despite being a wedding party: no noise, and someone even turned out the porch light for me. The next morning at breakfast three people joined them: I was prepared and had plenty of very fresh fruit and ham and mushroom quiche. Still, ten people do fill up the table. I peeped in from the kitchen: it looked as though they were having a good time. I silently blessed Mother and Granny's silver and china, of which there was plenty for ten.

One of my favorite pastimes was to do just this: watch my guests enjoying themselves. It wasn't so much about the money—well, it was, but that's not all it was. It was incredibly important to me that they were having fun. This group was like shooting fish in a barrel, because everyone knew everyone else and they were all excited about the wedding. When you have, say, three couples and a few tiny children, none of whom have met before, it's a greater challenge. I used to swan around with made-up errands when I heard someone coming downstairs—refilling the cream pitcher, checking to make sure there was plenty of water in the one-cup percolator, asking whether anyone needed something that wasn't on the sideboard—this gave me a chance to introduce people to one another, and if I was really wide awake, add a significant fact about them, such as "The Cranmers live in New Jersey also," or "The Bradfords are here for their son's commissioning in the National Guard."

If they made me really nervous—maybe with lots of teenaged boys—I'd say,

"I'll be out in the kitchen smashing crockery: if you need anything, just call me."

But mostly it was a pleasure simply to watch them enjoy and hear them make plans for a day in Marblehead or Boston.

People were in and out during the weekend of Melissa and Simon's wedding—all except for Aunt Sidney. Aunt Sidney was probably my favorite of Simon's kin. She lay in the hammock I have slung across the porch; it gives a good view of the harbor. She lay there whenever she wasn't involved in wedding festivities. Which was particularly understandable since, as the one single person at MoH, she'd drawn the bed in gloomy Steerage. She had a book with her, but as often as not she was just looking. She was delighted to talk but seemed equally happy by herself.

"You appear to enjoy doing this," she remarked one afternoon, as I came out to water the plants.

"I do, actually. As long as people are comfortable, I'm delighted to have them here."

"But," remarked Aunt Sidney, "Isn't it a little bit like—excuse me, but a little bit like being a *maid*? I mean, you have to feed us and do the dishes and change the sheets and empty the wastebaskets and all."

"It is definitely work, for sure. But it's all in your point of view. My late husband loved company, just loved it. He was never happier than when he had three or four people sleeping over. So I've been doing all the things you mention for years. The difference is that now I'm getting paid for it."

Aunt Sidney, acknowledging that there was something to that, returned to her book.

The wedding on Saturday occasioned another round of ironing and general pandemonium. Stuart couldn't find his belt and he was absolutely sure he'd had it the night before. Jeannine had forgotten to bring her black and gold scarf, which absolutely *made* her outfit.

"Not to worry," I said. "Wait till you see the black and gold scarf I've got for you."

Vivian needed a zillion tiny buttons buttoned up her back. I buttoned her up, then took pictures with everybody's cameras.

It was a lovely day, warm but not hot, with a gentle breeze. The wedding was at home, with a reception on the porch and in the yard afterwards. Apparently it all went beautifully. Lawrence, Simon's brother, told me he thought his brother was the cleverest and most successful man he had ever met. I was impressed: there seemed to be not a shred of envy, just the deep admiration of a younger brother. And everyone agreed Melissa was beautiful beyond compare. No surprise there.

As I got to know them a bit over the weekend, I more or less fell in love with all of them. I was hanging around in the kitchen Sunday afternoon, ironing pillowcases and napkins and wishing it were still Saturday and they weren't leaving, when Aunt Sidney banged on the door. There had been a dreadful storm somewhere out west and Logan was shy a number of planes, including theirs! They *weren't* leaving!

You could say, Be careful what you wish for, but my wish had been sincere. All but two stayed an extra day and caught a morning flight on Monday before the next round of guests. I had pulled out all the really nice leftovers from the previous days and added a quiche Lorraine and some extra bacon. I had a seat at the table and a second cup of coffee while they discussed the wedding. Hard to believe it had all gone off without a hitch, they marveled—but I think you can't really tell from the outside. My stepdaughter Liza wound up going down the aisle with her veil held on by paper clips at her wedding because neither her mother nor I had thought to bring bobby pins.

A wonderful experience such as this makes running a B & B all worthwhile. That's the way it's supposed to work. And these guests were smart and funny and nice. And best of all, they really loved the house, complimenting the layout, the view, the sturdy Victorian architecture. All of it warmed my heart—especially in light of my disappointment in Toby.

I didn't meet Simon, the bridegroom, till several years after the wedding. We ran into each other at a party where everyone had a nametag: he quickly realized who I was and thanked me for the lovely time his family had had at MoH. I thanked *him.*

"Simon, it was sheer pleasure, believe me. They were wonderful guests."

He also mentioned that he knew a classmate of mine from grade school. How he made the connection I don't know: it's been close to fifty years since we graduated from grade school and my name has changed. Clearly a clever man and maybe, just maybe, good enough for Melissa.

# CHAPTER 18

I've noted that people often left their phone chargers when they left Marble-head on Harbor. Please do not think this is all they left. Things I mailed to guests include a pillow; a brightly colored Hawaiian shirt (actually I don't think there's any other kind); lots of eyeglasses and sunglasses; prescription medication; underwear, male and female; a shoe; and an extremely large box of Muesli. It seems a little odd to bring your own cereal to a bed and breakfast.

A lot of guests leave stuff and apparently don't care if they never get it back. My Banana Republic t-shirt, for example. A gorgeous two-sided makeup mirror that plugs in so you can, if you wish, see every pore. A beautiful large black leather purse with silver trim from England—the strap had come loose from the silver ring that was holding it: the fix took me two minutes with my needle-nosed pliers. Of course I'm still using the purse. I think that particular guest had been to Saks and bought a replace-ment. But still.

Europeans in particular leave a lot, really a lot, of stuff so they won't have to carry it with them or have it confiscated—everything from fancy shampoo and conditioner to lotions, contact lens solution, and all man-ner of cosmetics. If you're traveling by plane you can rightly assume these things are going to be taken away. Many books, naturally—I learned how little I can deal with Jack Reacher novels. And many, many half-drunk bottles of wine and six-packs of beer. I'm still using a number of things that were left behind. Such are the perks of running a bed and breakfast.

Perks, yes. Then there's the dark side: Things You Really Didn't Want. One afternoon I was in the back hall carrying a load of clean laundry when I noticed something moving in the front hall. I'd opened the front door to let in a nice fresh breeze. It had also let in a young squirrel. You'd think the bird episode would've marked me for life. I guess some people are slow learners, and I do love fresh air.

I shouted and waved the laundry at him, but the squirrel was maybe too juvenile to have learned about humans. He just stared at me with black beady eyes. I ran at him. Of course he ran into the living room, and then into the kitchen. I began shutting doors, but didn't get to the back stairs before he had nipped up to the second floor. I had rooms all ready for guests the next day, Friday, and had left all the doors open to catch the breeze and look welcoming. The squirrel ran into Starboard Home, naturally. Before I could open the big glass sliding door he had taken fright and scrambled under the bed.

Miserably I tried to poke around under the king-size bed and startle him into coming out. This did not work. I opened the glass slider and shut the bedroom door hoping he'd find his way out. An older couple was coming in to Starboard Home the next day and I really didn't want him greeting them. Several hours passed, during which I made banana bread with another of domestic goddess Susan's recipes; then I went upstairs to check whether he'd gone. The minute I opened the door I heard a lot of scrabbling and scuffling under the bed. Alas, he had gone nowhere.

Why is it that little rabbits are adorable but squirrels, big or little, are not? I didn't spend much time wondering: I got a broom and began pushing it around under the bed. I pushed the broom way down deep—he ran the other way. I tried to sort of scoop him out with it—he cowered somewhere near the wall. I got annoyed and stupidly began yelling at him. As if he could understand any of this. While I was cursing and fussing, he ran out of the room and down the back stairs.

Luckily I had left all the doors downstairs closed: all I had to do was close that one door at the top of the back stairs and he was mine! I closed it and continued down the back stairs. It was satisfying to know that at least he wasn't going to get into any of the guests' rooms, even if he and I had to share living quarters in the kitchen and family room. I wasn't going to open any of those doors until he was *gone*. Like, totally gone.

I got my dinner: a peanut butter sandwich with lettuce, cheese, and onions. (You can do this when you're single.) Realizing that peanut butter might be the very thing to lure him out, I put a little dish of it near the outside door. Slowly, I heard him coming toward the dish. I pounced on him—too soon. He eluded me and ran behind the sofa. I promised myself to leave him alone and settled down to watch a "Call the Midwife" episode I'd taped. I love "Call the Midwife": I cry every time a baby is born: it feels really good. And everyone there is so well intentioned and kind. Like somewhere anyone would want to live. Probably squirrel-free, too.

Toby's nightly call came at the end of the program. Amazingly, we always had quite a lot to talk about from one day to the next.

"How was your day, sweetie?"

"I hope yours was better." I told him about my unsuccessful pursuit of the squirrel.

"That's awful! But I think I can top it: I've got carpenter ants all through the clapboards on the front of the house. The men were about to start painting the house when a gang of these creatures made their appearance. It's going to cost me a fortune on top of the paint job!"

My heart went out to him. He'd been worrying about the cost of painting the house, and now this too.

"Anything I can do?"

"You could come down here. And if you could also get rid of the dratted woodpecker who wakes me up every morning, that would help a lot, too."

"I'll see what I can do." Clearly the animals were waging war on us, and they were winning.

When I went upstairs to bed, there was a kerfuffle behind me and the wretched squirrel charged out into the upstairs hall, then went to earth again in Starboard Home. How unspeakably dumb of me to let him through the door! Why couldn't he have run into my room, or my office, or even Amidships? Why take the absolute best room, no doubt depositing squirrel droppings all over it? He'd probably begun to feel at home there. I was so tired from chasing him around that I decided to give up. I left the door to Starboard Home open and put a dish of peanut butter on the back stairs about midway down. He was bound to be hungry.

I slept badly and woke Friday morning feeling not great. I remembered an unwanted visitor was causing this not-great feeling. I went down to get myself some breakfast.

The previous night, I'd left a bag of trash on the floor beside the stove—all the trash from the various bedrooms and baths. As my eyes focused, I saw a little gray tail sticking out of the top. Eww. He was probably helping himself to Lord knows what from the guests' trash. Some of them liked to eat in their rooms, not always thoughtfully. (I'd once found one of my silver forks in the waste basket of Starboard Home, someone having helped him- or herself to it and disposed of it in a distinctly unthoughtful manner.)

I tiptoed up and closed the bag quickly. There wasn't a sound from inside. Carefully I opened the bag just a crack. He was still there and he hadn't moved. I tentatively poked him. He lay completely still.

When I realized he was dead, I couldn't believe it. And I still don't get it. Was he so little that he didn't take his head out of the plastic bag, thus suffocating himself? Don't animals have good instincts around self-preservation? Or had he tried to eat something that isn't good for squirrels—like nail polish remover, or shampoo? I'll never know. All part of the job, I guess.

Early that afternoon, an interesting threesome arrived: a couple escorting a third person, a middle-aged or maybe elderly man. They asked if they might look at the rooms. As we walked through, the couple kept encouraging the gentleman to look at the paintings, or to admire the view, or whatever. They seemed to be talking to him as if he was maybe a bit lacking, or had had a stroke or something. I couldn't quite figure it out. For his part, he seemed to have almost no affect: he answered everything very politely, but with no particular enthusiasm. Everything was fine; nothing seemed special.

"Look at this, Joe! You'd love being in this room!" said the woman, a little too brightly. She seemed to be trying to cheer him up. "Just look at all the boats!" We were in Starboard Home overlooking the harbor. She sounded as if she were talking to a child. Actually, a self-respecting child would have been insulted. But Joe didn't seem to mind. He agreed there were a lot of boats. They left, assuring me Joe would visit soon. I told them I'd be delighted.

Three o'clock came and a very sweet couple arrived: a young lady and a much older man. I took them to the room they'd registered for, Seaview, on the third floor. She seemed very protective of him. When we got to the room, she said,

"I'm not sure Nathan can stay in here. It doesn't look as though there's a fire escape." She went on to explain: "He was in a terrible fire a few years back—he was asleep, and he barely got out alive. Ever since, he's been terrified of fire."

"That makes sense. I'm sorry you had to go through that," I told Nathan. "But I have something that may help." I reached under the bed and pulled out the fire escape ladder that Larry had bought at one of those Job Lots places. It hooked over a windowsill and you climbed down a set of metal rungs attached by chains. Luckily we'd never needed it: now we did need it, for Nathan's peace of mind. It appeared to be well built and very sturdy.

"This will get you to the deck below, and from there you can step out on the roof and either jump or go down by way of the beech tree. I'll show it to you after you get settled."

"Could I see it now?" Nathan asked.

"Of course." We walked downstairs, went out onto the deck from my study, and peered over the roof at a tall, robust beech tree growing about a foot out from the roof. Nathan said he was confident this would do the trick. I'd have relocated him a floor down, but Starboard Home and Amidships were both taken. Fortunately, we had no fires that weekend and didn't have to test out the ladder-and-tree system.

The third couple arrived and were duly waved into Starboard Home. They had visited before, staying in Amidships, and were delighted to have upgraded.

With a full house and no fire or squirrels, we all slept well. The next morning at breakfast, I was serving Thomas's English muffins, among other things. Nancy, in Amidships, commented on how good they were: in fact, she tossed a second muffin into the toaster. When all the muffins were gone, she appeared at the door to the kitchen with the bread basket.

"Do you have any more muffins? I'm afraid we've eaten them all."

The royal "we." I gave her the four I had left, and was amazed to see that, while only one other person had a muffin, Nancy made away with the other three. "We," indeed! She had eaten five English muffins by herself! Does anyone do that? Well, besides people with eating disorders. I found myself feeling vaguely envious: I don't think I've ever eaten as many English muffins as I wanted. Lucky we had the banana bread I'd made to serve the next day. And the weekend passed uneventfully.

Well, except for an odd email I received Saturday night. A man named Matthias wanted to hold a week's business retreat in MoH in a month's time. He'd be bringing five people with him and wondered if I could accommodate him. There would be no problem if they needed to share beds and/or baths. And please let him know how much of a deposit I wanted: he'd send it right away. He wrote as if English wasn't his native language and signed himself my humble servant.

Oh, boy! The dollar signs sparkling in my eyes, I added up how much that would net me. It looked like something over $5,000. Naturally, I was delighted. I emailed him immediately to say the rooms were free and if he could send me $2,500 by check, I would hold them for him. He was delighted and said he'd send the check right away.

The check arrived. It was in the amount of $25,000! Oh, no—how could he get it so wrong? I emailed him back and told him the deposit was actually just a tenth of this amount and I would tear this check up. Please could he send me a check for $2,500?

His email arrived promptly. Not to worry, he said: just deposit his check and send him a check of mine for the amount over $2,500. Well, that would work. As I started to comply, I suddenly felt a little jolt—maybe you could call it a sixth sense—that told me something wasn't right. I called Charlie.

"You got it, Mumz. Good for you. It's a scam, all right, and a fairly popular one, because it works for all kinds of activities, not just B & Bs. You deposit that check in your account and send him one for the difference, or $22,500. A week later the bank tells you his check has bounced higher than a superball, you're out $22,500, and you never hear from him again."

A close shave. And I was disappointed, and sad—not just over losing the money, but because it had sounded like an interesting week. I wrote him an email telling him I had no intention of doing as he suggested, and that I was tearing up his check. I also told him he was a scammer and that I didn't want to hear from him again.

He wrote back: "What? You think I am some scamming? You have cut me to the heart!"

I burst out laughing. Thank goodness for that warning bell, or whatever you want to call it. I could have lost quite a lot of money. And, as usual, thank goodness for Charlie also.

I continued to get messages from folks trying to pull similar scams. I still do. Here is perhaps the most unusual:

RESERVATION REQUEST
6/24/20—9:02 AM
Chivo chink
To undisclosed-recipients: Blind copy bburck@comcast.net
ROOM REQUEST
Dear sir/madam,
Kindly inform me if there is availability of 10 Luxurious Suite

(single) in your accommodation facility that will sleep 10 guest for
duration of 10 days that is from 15th to 25th September, 2017.
However, if you have available room as requested, sincerely get back
to me with the price rate of total rooms including of breakfast,
dinner and tax.
Best regards.

You can't make this stuff up. At least I can't. I think Chivo chink is an
amazing name, if that's what it's supposed to be. I sincerely got back to him
and told him I knew this game. I didn't tell him that even if he was on the
level (just possible) I was not cooking *dinner* every night for 10 guests. The
scary thing is that I might have fallen for it—and I guess quite a few people
do. I never heard from Chivo chink again.

Joe called—the odd gentleman with the minimal affect—and made a
reservation for Starboard Home. He duly arrived the next weekend with a
very small suitcase and a bottle of Scotch in a brown paper bag. (I peeked
in the bag and saw the label, which said Chivas Regal.)

I gave him the tour again, in case he'd forgotten about the little refrigerator for ice cubes, etc., and reminded him the deck was for his private
use. He asked if I would have a drink with him there.

Frankly, I missed that deck, and I agreed happily. I brought an ice
bucket and a board with some cheese and crackers and we settled in.

"Did you grow up in Massachusetts?" I asked.

"No. I am half Lebanese: I grew up in Beirut."

"They know how to do food in Lebanon. We have Le Bistro here
in town, which serves quite a few Lebanese, or Lebanese-inspired, dishes.
Maybe you can try it while you're here."

The conversation went along in this vein. Some of his oddness came
perhaps from not being a native, though I hadn't picked it up on his previous visit.

Then he seemed to gather a little energy and asked, "Will you sleep
with me?"

Only a little energy. His mood actually didn't alter much.

"I'm sorry, but sleeping with isn't one of the perks of this B & B. They
may do things differently elsewhere." I dealt with him fairly gently, as I felt
he was emotionally fragile. "It was nice of you to ask."

He seemed unsurprised and not terribly affected one way or the other.
I wonder whether the couple that brought him had suggested this. He

himself didn't seem to have much investment in the idea. We topped off our drinks and watched the sun set, then said pleasant good nights and went to our separate beds.

# CHAPTER 19

Things moved along smoothly for a while. I spoke with Toby every night and had a lot of guests. Jill and Sandy were returning, which delighted me: they'd come the first summer and seemed to appreciate the same things I did about the North Shore: they went to Salem to see the world-class Peabody-Essex Museum, not the creepy witch dungeons, tacky tarot card and crystal pendant shops, and godawful statue of that TV witch Samantha sitting on a moonbeam. (This is not just inappropriate: it's a very poorly done statue.) These all reference Salem's most shameful moments: I think it's a crime to make money off them.

I was also delighted that Jill and Sandy had invited their son John and his girlfriend Lillian to join them at the house. Well, at least until I heard the news: John and Lillian were vegan. This in itself was no problem: Jill and Sandy, however, were gluten-free. Have you ever tried to cook a gluten-free *and* vegan breakfast? I didn't think so. It can be done—if you are careful to omit anything with gluten (wheat, and sometimes barley, oats, and rye), eggs, and dairy products. That's milk, butter, and cheese. Toby likes mince pie for breakfast and suggested this might please everyone: well, as long as I skipped the eggs and made a crust without flour or butter… Right. I'd been cooking gluten-free for years. I just needed to adapt the recipes to cut out the eggs and dairy.

Another couple with two little boys came in Friday afternoon to occupy the third floor. I was getting kind of cocky, swanning around upstairs that afternoon replacing rolls of toilet paper in the bathrooms and congratulating myself on coping so well with all four bedrooms and three baths in use. That kind of thinking is so asking for trouble.

A voice downstairs yelled, "I am Tovar! I have a reservation!" She had a strong accent, maybe Scandinavian.

I don't care if you're Xena, warrior princess, I muttered. You don't have a reservation *here*. Once again, practically begging for trouble. I bounced down the stairs with a polite smile on my face. A very large, very blonde, very Scandinavian woman in white short shorts stood in the front hall.

"Hi!" I said. "Glad to see you—but I wonder if you might possibly be confusing me with Harbor House." I went on, perhaps a little glibly, "Lots of people do. I actually have a full house tonight."

"Oh?" responded Tovar. She read from a note in her large, probably neck-breaking hand: "Becky Burckmyer? 15 Corinthian Lane? Marblehead on Harbor?"

Whoops. I began to tremble, probably visibly. "Oh, my God. I've done something awful. I am so sorry! I don't have you down in my book anywhere." It was obvious to both of us just who was confused.

"You don't have me in your book?" said Tovar. She made the word "book" sound like a bad word. "And yet I call you from Copenhagen and make this reservation in April, for my husband and me and our two daughters. Two nights," she added, in case I was still having trouble focusing on the gravity of the situation. I was having no trouble. In fact, I realized immediately what had happened.

When I had guests from overseas wanting to make reservations, I usually took their credit card numbers because they couldn't write me checks as the guests here in the United States did. It was something of a sham, because I didn't have the ability to process credit cards (just never got around to it), but it was a way to keep them honest, because I had their number, so to speak. Unfortunately, I normally confirmed the customer's reservation when I received a check. This procedure, or non-procedure, had allowed Tovar to slip through the cracks and be lost.

Why had I ever thought I was in control of the situation? Why had I ever thought I could run a bed and breakfast? I was such an unbelievable screw-up.

"I have the Starboard Home room," my new guest added helpfully. Jill and Sandy's room. Of course. I felt as though my brain would explode. "I am so sorry, Tovar. This is obviously my mistake, and I feel absolutely terrible about it. That room isn't available, but you and your husband can have my room and the girls can sleep on the sofa bed—they'll have a dynamite view." I was babbling, I was so frightened. Doing wrong by a customer brought out all the hobgoblins again. I felt awful for her. Plus, she was really big. "You'll have to share the little bath downstairs with me but just for one night—and your visit will be entirely at my expense."

"Don't worry too much," Tovar astonished me by saying. I think maybe the trembling had impressed her. "Mistakes do happen. We will figure this out." She actually patted me on the arm. "Maybe you let my girls go to the bathroom? Then we go to town."

"Of course! And I'll make the beds: everything will be ready when you get back."

"That will be fine," Tovar declared. She stepped to the door and yelled for her family. In they trooped, two adolescent girls and their father. I pointed the way to the bathroom and hared upstairs to rip the sheets off my bed (I had only one set of queen-size sheets, a gift from the linen closet of Barb, my B & B sitter, who spent her leisure time thinking up nice things to do for me).

Refreshed, the family left to tour Old Town while I frantically laundered sheets and made up the sofa bed. I improvised a sherry carafe, added several soft drinks, and put out lots of trail mix in the two rooms—placating as well as possible. I was still pretty scared.

I ran downstairs to throw the sheets into the dryer on Very Very High and headed for the bathroom we were going to be sharing to put some extra towels in for the family. I opened the door and stopped in my tracks. The bathroom was a wreck. Toilet paper hung in festoons on toilet, sink, and roller. Soaking wet towels lay in puddles on the floor. The cake soap was swimming, the pump soap empty on its side. The girls evidently were not used to picking up after themselves; or else they do things differently in Copenhagen. I sighed and began to clean up. It was going to be a long night.

I don't know if you've ever torn the sheets off a bed, washed them, dried them, and put them back on the bed without stopping for breath: it takes a toll.

The phone rang. What fresh hell? I thought. But it was Tovar. They'd stopped for a drink at the Harbor Light Inn and liked it so much they'd decided to stay there instead! I apologized again—and again— thanked her for being so fabulous, hung up and collapsed, giddy with fatigue and relief.

Did I mention that Tovar's family was black? Thank the gentle heavens I hadn't seen them, and Tovar knew this, before I said No Room at the Inn. I could see the headlines in The Marblehead Reporter: Racist Hostess

Denies Admission to Black Family, etc. As it was, I checked Trip Advisor for weeks to see whether Tovar had lashed into me publicly for my horrible bookkeeping. God love her, she never did. Once again, I felt I'd cheated the hangman, and I was distressed. I was holding onto my teardown house, but I wasn't doing right by all my guests. Or would-be guests. Once again, I wasn't good at my job. And maybe my job wasn't so good for me.

That night I set to work to make breakfast squares, an MoH specialty, which are made with wheat germ—oops, delete that. Gluten-free flour, vegetable oil, molasses, and egg substitute went into the bowl, and the resulting concoction, complete with carrots, nuts, and raisins went into a pan and baked for 20 minutes. The result looked beautiful, but the next morning when I cut the squares, they weren't square. In fact, they lacked any structural integrity whatsoever. Jill was sweet: she insisted on taking a piece and ate it with a knife and fork. The others, perhaps frightened by their appearance, skipped them altogether. I couldn't blame them, though the darned things actually tasted pretty good. (The secret ingredient is the molasses: blended with the fruit, nuts, and carrots, it's memorable.)

Before the next breakfast, I laid in a store of cheese substitute, vegan nutrition bars, and vegan sausage. The gluten-free bread for toasting had eggs in it, I realized later, so I earmarked that for Jill and Sandy only, and a jolly breakfast was had by all. Note: When they left, I stuck the cheese, bars, and sausage in John's backpack. Never again. All were horrible.

Saturday Jill and Sandy took the young people to "do" Salem; they checked out museums, the House of Seven Gables—again the good stuff— and ate dinner in Salem. When they got back, I was in the living room swapping empty liqueur bottles for at least semi-full ones.

"Becky, I was wondering," said Sandy, after Jill had gone upstairs. He pointed to the monster rectangular grand piano. It had taken seven men to haul it up the front stairs. Miraculously, both the steps and the men survived. "Would you have any interest in selling that?"

"You want to buy the piano?" I was incredulous. Not only is the piano ugly, with huge carved rosewood legs, it also sounds terrible because, as I mentioned, it won't stay in tune. Husband Larry had fallen in love with it, who knows why, and I'd given in.

"No, no. The little statue."

A bronze nude, maybe 16 inches long, reclined on the piano. I'd always thought she was gorgeous: someone really good had created her. I'd tried without success to read the name on the plinth. She had the lovely verdigris patina of old bronze, gray-green except for her breasts, which a generation of men (I assume it was men) had caressed, leaving them bright as gold. I'd been curious about her ever since I saw her.

"Oh, gosh, Sandy. I don't know. She's something Larry bought on his travels—I guess I have kind of a nostalgic attachment to her."

"Well, as it happens, she was done by a turn-of-the-century English sculptor who's very collectible." He gave a name that wasn't familiar to me but was clearly, in hindsight, the name on the pedestal.

"I went on the Internet to see what he's currently fetching at auction—it's usually between four and eight thousand pounds. I'll give you ten thousand dollars for her."

My heart rate shot into the stratosphere. That was some real money! I mumbled something incoherent and fled, first to Google the sculptor, who fetched just what Sandy had reported, then to contact my two children. Their reactions were identical, swift, and predictable: "Mother, have you lost your mind? Take the money and run. And while you're at it, what else can you sell?"

Sentimental little darlings. I went downstairs and told Sandy I was sure Larry would appreciate a fellow collector's giving the little nude lady a home where she'd be appreciated for what she was—in fact, a collector's item. Sandy wrote me a check and bagged her up in a heavy canvas bag I gave him, still more or less in shock. Me, I mean. Sandy took it all in stride.

I told Toby about it when he called that night. He congratulated me, then asked, "How would you feel if you found out Sandy had sold her for twenty thousand?"

"Delighted for him, actually. If it weren't for him, I'd never have known what I had sitting on the piano. I didn't even deserve her. And in the space of one hour, I'm $10,000 richer."

I couldn't resist mentioning the exchange to Sandy and Jill. Sandy laughed. "Becky, I'm a collector, not an investor. Now that I've got her, I have no plans to let her go."

"It's true," Jill added. "He's been talking about her ever since we were here last year."

Not only lovely people, but by far the most profitable guests I ever had.

# CHAPTER 20

And then came the Di Santises, for whom I was completely unprepared. As if *any*one could be prepared for the Di Santises. I should have realized, when they called to ask if they could come have a look at Marblehead on Harbor, that they'd be something out of the ordinary. Most people were satisfied to look at the pictures of the house and harbor on the website. Renata Di Santis was not most people.

"My mother, my sister, and I would like to visit. We are planning a one-week stay in the Marblehead area and your house looks right for us, but we can't be sure until we get a good look in person. We're coming from Cohasset. We could be there tomorrow after lunch—probably around two o'clock." Renata spoke in a husky voice that reminded me of cigarettes and whisky—or maybe the heroine of a 1940s noir movie.

Of course, I told them. I'd look forward to meeting them.

They were late. Very late. It was a Saturday and Charlie had a date with me in the basement: he'd rented a Dumpster and was hurling much of the basement into it, but he had some questions for me, and the arrival of three women on his time didn't appeal to him. He greeted the Di Santis ladies with an evil grace, then vanished.

"We would've been here earlier, but we got lost in East Boston," said Renata, clearly the leader of the little group. She gave a booming laugh, at odds with her petite, tiny frame. "This is my mother, Elena." The mother, somewhere fairly far north of 80, stared hard at me with shoe-button black eyes, took a seat on a dining room chair, and didn't budge for the rest of the visit. She said never a word, just continued to stare. I couldn't tell whether she liked what she saw or not. She wore a heavy green coat of some synthetic fur, which must have been horribly hot, but she refused to remove it.

"And my sister, Benedetta," Renata added, as something of an afterthought. A pretty, thin lady of perhaps 50 smiled and gave me a little self-deprecatory wave. Evidently she was used to being marginalized. Renata, on the other hand, was bigger than life. No one was going to marginalize Renata. She had the most arresting huge brown eyes and dramatic, dark wavy hair that kept threatening to fall over one eye, and she was dressed in a lot of gauzy items. Her voice was loud and about an octave below middle C. She was the younger sister, I discovered, but I doubt most people would realize this.

Renata and Benedetta walked all over the house, examining every room—it took a long time—and pronounced Starboard Home the perfect venue for their week's vacation. I raised a silent prayer of thanks to Ben for the ensuite bathroom, which ensured Elena didn't have to negotiate the staircase if she got up during the night.

"I'll put a rollaway bed in the room, since there are three of you," I suggested.

"Oh, don't bother. It's a king-size bed: that's big enough for all of us." My face must have registered the shock I felt, for Renata added, "We're a very close family."

"It's true," Benedetta added. "Renata was engaged once, but when she realized she'd have to leave us, she broke it off. Isn't that so, Renata?"

"He wasn't right for me, anyway," Renata yelled. "But realizing I'd have to leave Papa, Mamma, and Benedetta was the last straw."

Charlie came in and announced that he needed his mother back. I gave him a dark look, but the ladies took it cheerfully, and roared off in their Cadillac Seville.

Renata called the next day: they would take the room and be there two months hence. I lived in fear.

At last the day came on which the Di Santises were to take possession of Starboard Home. They called ahead to ask if they could come a little early. I had some people in the room, but they'd be leaving by noon. It wouldn't be terribly hard to have the room ready by one o'clock: I would just have to move faster than usual. So I moved, changing the big bed, dusting, vacuuming, emptying the wastebaskets, and getting rid of the trash sitting around. People always left maps and brochures, and sometimes not-very-appetizing leftover food. Because the bathroom was so little, it was relatively easy to clean. I swished the toilet bowl fiercely with Lysol and brush, scrubbed the sink and tub with Comet, replaced the used towels with clean ones, and washed the bathroom floor.

I put fresh flowers on the bureau, refreshed the sherry carafe, got more trail mix, napkins, and Lindt truffles. I checked the big glass double doors to the porch to be sure the birds hadn't hit them. Naturally they had. I grabbed a sponge and tidied the doors up, then stood back and admired. The colors of the room were based on the king-sized bedspread and pillow shams, which were very pretty. Sarah had helped me pick them out of the L. L. Bean catalog: she has a wonderful eye: I don't think of L.L. Bean as a decorator store. You may remember I had also painted the closet and bathroom door panels in corresponding colors. Four curtain panels of the same deep red hung at the sliding doors. I had cushions from Walmart in deep red for the chaise longue on the porch. The whole effect is pretty attractive, and I was proud of it.

It was one o'clock. Time for the ladies. I grabbed a yogurt and made sure Seaview, to be occupied by someone else that afternoon, was in good shape. Then I sat down to pay some bills and answer my email.

One-thirty came, then two o'clock. Hurry up and wait, of course: I could've taken my time. Renata was probably roaming East Boston again. Three o'clock. The businesswoman who'd reserved Seaview arrived. No sign of the Di Santises. Then, finally, at 4:30 I heard the sound of an engine being revved painfully, looked out the window, and saw Renata and Co. emerging from the Seville.

We embraced, shouting greetings. (If someone else is shouting, I start shouting too. Renata quickly got me going.) They were actually pretty adorable, and I was delighted to see them. It had occurred to me that they just might've decided to do something utterly different, like go to Newport, so it was also a relief.

I don't think I have ever seen so much stuff in my life as Renata and Benedetta began carrying into the house. I ran down and grabbed a couple of suitcases: it wasn't even a tenth of what they had with them. Pillows, and quilts (quilts? It was July), and heaps of clothes on hangers, and photographs in frames, and baskets full of who knows what came pouring into the house. I had turned the air conditioner on in Starboard Home, and we put Mamma Elena in a comfortable chair. She tended to stay put wherever you set her down, like a well-behaved plant, so I didn't worry about her.

Starboard Home began to take on a distinctly Di Santis personality.

Various items were positioned around the room, most prominently a number of pictures of a very attractive man in the prime of life.

"Who is this?" I asked, indicating the photos.

Renata approached my ear and attempted to whisper: "Don't say anything. That's Pappa. It upsets her" (she tilted her head towards her mother) "if we mention Him."

Evidently the photographs didn't bother her. "I'm so sorry. How long has he been gone?"

"Eight years," she replied. Elena looked up. "I think she heard me," Renata boomed, pulling a sad face.

Mr. Di Santis was obviously a person with some serious charisma. Eight years! And they had brought all these pictures of him along on their holiday. And still had to tiptoe around their mother when speaking of him. I was impressed.

The unpacking finally accomplished, the Di Santises came down to the living room to drink some wine and plan for the evening. They settled themselves, took a look at the notebook of the menus of restaurants in Marblehead and nearby, and took off for dinner.

I was just about to go up to bed when the Di Santises returned. Everyone had had a lovely meal except Mamma Elena, and Renata's nose was badly out of joint. The problem seemed to be that there was too much food for their mother. It had really taken her appetite, hollered Renata, and the management should have told them ahead of time how large the portion was going to be.

"Did you consider bringing what she couldn't eat back here?" I asked. I had shown them the little refrigerator in the dining room where guests could keep whatever. "You could always have it for lunch or something." I was perplexed that this was clearly perceived as a lapse on the part of the restaurant.

"Well, yes, but you know. That doesn't really address the problem," Renata told me. This restaurant was going to be on her bad list for a long time, that much was clear. They said goodnight and headed upstairs, Renata still grumbling.

The next morning my single guest, Donnie, and I were startled to see the Di Santis girls appear for breakfast in their nightgowns. They were beautiful and modest Laura Ashley-type gowns, cotton, trimmed with ribbons and lace, with long sleeves and hems to the floor. But they were nightgowns. I'd once had a guest who came down each morning with her hair in rollers, but I hadn't seen this before. It gave a new meaning to the phrase "Your home away from home." They helped themselves to the buffet and sat down to talk.

Donnie and I were regaled with the story of Renata's doctor, who was, Benedetta assured us, secretly in love with Renata, since he had looked at her *very* hard as he reminded her always to take her medicine. Very, very hard. Benedetta looked at us meaningfully. Renata was diabetic, and he obviously was terribly concerned that something might happen to her if she wasn't careful with the prescriptions.

"Oh, good Lord!" cried Renata. "You can't be serious. Of course he's interested in me, but only, I guarantee you, as a patient. He's a very important man! Why would he bother with me?"

"I can think of a reason," Benedetta answered, staring at Renata. "If he *cared*. And how do you know he doesn't?"

"I give up. What can you do with a sister like this?" Renata appealed to me. Mamma ate her breakfast, apparently unmoved.

The week went on in much the same way. A lot of shopping took place: the ladies were charmed by the little shops in town and brought home trinkets and clothing each day. I had to admire them: their lives were so different from mine, and not what I could've dealt with. Yet they so obviously loved and cared about one another and seemed truly happy and contented. As the weekend drew near, they asked whether they might stay one more night and leave on Sunday. I had no one coming into the room and gladly agreed.

Saturday came and so did Toby. The Di Santis ladies were predictably charmed, and Toby enjoyed their colorful affect. He was stunned, of course, by Nightgowns on Parade, and almost as much by Renata's booming laugh. They told us they were going off to have lunch with a distant relative who lived on the other side of the harbor, and they took off laden with gifts and dressed to the nines. When they returned, they were thrilled at how hospitable he had been and ecstatic over his beautiful house. They seemed to have a big sweet spot: they enjoyed everything they did.

This lasted until Sunday, checkout being at 11:00 a.m. and the Di Santises in no way ready to go. I had someone coming into the room that afternoon. Remembering the stuff they had carried into the place, I thought I had better help them move out. Toby had cleverly developed an errand in Swampscott and was nowhere to be seen. We repeated the moving-in process in reverse, Renata becoming remarkably shrewish as Benedetta did her best to organize and remove their effects.

"What can you do with a sister like this?" Renata demanded again, this time not very pleasantly. Mamma Elena sat quietly. I thought she looked sad as Benedetta fell apart under Renata's bullying. The Di Santis cup of joy had definitely stopped overflowing. I feel that way myself sometimes on Sundays. And, of course, it was the end of their vacation. (Both ladies had full-time administrative jobs.)

Toby returned, his quest for screws or whatever it was successful, and offered his services. We finally finished loading the car, came back up the porch stairs and saw Renata pouring half a brandy bottle into her water bottle. (I kept hoping people would drink the liqueurs up, so I wasn't unhappy, but this worried me a little. I didn't want the ladies coming to grief on the Southeast Expressway.)

We said our goodbyes and watched them climb into the Cadillac. The usual revving (grinding) of the engine commenced. As we waved from the porch, we saw Renata yank the top off the water bottle—With. Her. Teeth—and take a healthy swig. We stifled giggles (Toby) and gasps (me). With a liberal spewing of gravel, the Cadillac tore backward out of the driveway. And they were gone. I miss them.

# CHAPTER 21

Toby came for a weekend in early August. He'd been coming more frequently, which was nice; our relationship seemed to be getting back on track. The activity at MoH was particularly frenetic: people were putting stuff in our supposedly "private" fridge at the back of the house; others were eating lobster on the porch and loudly asking where they should put the shells; and a child kept asking, "Miss Becky, will you play with me?" And there were the beds, and the laundry, and the breakfasts. And, of course, the bathroom floors.

I heard Toby answer the phone, "Downton Abbey, Carson speaking."

It was funny, but it spoke to a deeper truth: in fact, as Aunt Sidney had observed, we were servants, and busy ones at that. Like the staff at Downton Abbey, we were relegated to certain areas of the house, and they weren't the nicest areas. We rarely even stepped out onto the porch unless the guests invited us. Hearing Toby's greeting, I felt disenfranchised, the truth being that my much-loved home wasn't entirely mine. When he left, I was glad for him.

But the worst was yet to come. A lovable friend from the days when we had children in the same school in Marblehead had a son getting married in August. She was planning the rehearsal dinner and had asked over the winter whether she could have this bunfight on the porch and in the yard.

"I'll do all the cooking, I'll buy all the drinks," Sally said. "I'll rent tables for the yard, I'll get the silver and the plates and napkins. And I'll put it all together. I'm guessing we'll have about 35 people. You won't have to do anything but provide the venue. Oh, and save all the rooms for the bride's out-of-town family."

It sounded kind of wonderful: as I said before, I love weddings. So I disregarded the advice I'd been given to say No to wedding parties and said Yes, and, knowing that as a single mom she didn't have a lot of cash to throw around, named a very low dollar figure for rental of the kitchen, porch, and yard. After all, she was a friend. August came, and Sally called. She did indeed need all four rooms for four days. The guest list for the dinner had swelled to 80. Well, all right. It was her show, after all. When Toby called, he suggested that, particularly as a lot of the guests were young, I should request that Sally order up at least two Port-A-Potties. A great idea: my plumbing, dating from the early 20th century, is cranky and unpredictable, and young people drink beer. Sally agreed enthusiastically.

I made sure the kitchen was clear of as much of my gear as possible, given that I had to fix breakfast for eight each morning. I also made as much room as possible in the refrigerators in both kitchen and basement.

The last Friday in August was D-Day. Toby wisely decided to stay away. The eight guests rolled in late the night before. They were marvelous: one family, but a mix of Greeks and Argentinians, young and old, all of them ready to party.

I had gotten into the spirit of things and noticed the yard looked sort of sad. Why not take the party money and spruce it up a bit? I couldn't do much about the grass, but Sally had assured me the tables would cover its sins. Reggie, chatty blond gardener extraordinaire, sped over on his baby blue Vespa when I called and readily agreed to help. He borrowed my friend Jean's gorgeous around-the-pool plants (she was away but had given us her permission), and, with an infusion of mulch and late-summer annuals in lavender and white, made the gardens and urns look more than respectable. It gave me a terrific boost. (I was going to need it.)

Friday morning I served breakfast and got to know the guests a little. They were wonderfully friendly and quite glamorous. The men had tightly tailored suits and pointy-toed European shoes, the women were fantastically thin and beautifully dressed and made up. They had decided against renting cars, but had made fast friends with Andreas the Witch City taxi driver, who duly arrived to help them tour the North Shore. Sally came over in the afternoon with flowers and food. The kitchen was immediately and totally taken over. Pots boiled away on the stove, hors d'oeuvres sat in rows awaiting garniture, beer stood in galvanized tubs of ice. Meanwhile, a rental company was setting up 11 round tables on the lawn.

"We're up to 90 people!" Sally exclaimed happily. Good Lord, I thought. There was no sign of a Port-A-Potty.

"Sally, did you rent —"

"Can't talk now," Sally said. I realized she was on her cell phone calling for more flowers. It didn't matter. If she hadn't ordered toilets, we were on our own: I didn't really want to know. I made a mental note that the flag needed to come down at sunset as usual. Maybe I could ask a guest to take over this chore so I could remain upstairs: I didn't feel I belonged at the rehearsal dinner, though Sally and the guests had cordially invited me.

Six-thirty came, and miraculously Sally had everything in good order and at the ready. Little quiches and endive piped with salmon mousse began appearing on the porch tables, and the stiletto heels of guests could be heard clicking down the stairs indoors and up the front stairs outdoors. Thank goodness it was a beautiful evening. I fled upstairs with a sandwich and connected with my book.

Soon I heard sounds of revelry, which continued to increase. It sounded like a wonderful time, and it increased in volume by the minute. The yacht club cannons went off, announcing sunset: I had forgotten to ask George, the up-for-anything father of the bride, to take the flag down. Darn. I sprang from the bed and zipped down the stairs. I looked out the picture window onto the porch, and almost lost it.

It's hard to describe, but what I saw out there was the life I had lived and didn't live any longer. All of those lovely people standing out there, talking, eating, drinking, and enjoying the harbor view. The way Larry and I had entertained, which now seemed so long ago. It was like looking at ghosts. Or maybe I was the ghost. I experienced a sense of intense loss, of my life passing me by; it was a powerful feeling. My wonderful house felt even more like Not My House, and I an onlooker, not the real owner.

This lasted only a minute: I whisked outside and, saying polite Hellos as I pushed my way through the crowd, gathered the flag in my arms and disappeared from this place where I didn't feel I belonged.

As the evening wore on, I began to hear the tramp of feet up and down the stairs, as the beers worked their way through the guests' systems. Clearly the plumbing system was imperiled. Furthermore, a couple of the in-house guests, who'd been told they had private baths, came complaining to me. This seemed unfair, as the people using the bathrooms were wedding guests also—and it wasn't my fault Sally hadn't arranged for outdoor facilities. I did my best to assuage them, praying all the time that we wouldn't have a disaster: they had no idea how much more awful it could be. I pictured water — or worse — all over the rug in Starboard Home: it didn't bear thinking of. Fortunately, I had brought a bottle of Scotch upstairs with me, to which I liberally applied myself. Miraculously, all four toilets bore up bravely, and the worst did not in fact happen.

Gradually, the noise died down. The last of the party guests went away; Sally came upstairs to my room.

"Omigosh, it was such a terrific party! I promise I'll be back bright and early to clean up. Don't worry about a thing."

I wasn't wild about this, but I didn't have much choice. She was the groom's mother and she needed her sleep.

The house guests were cheerful at breakfast: it had indeed been a fabulous party. But my first view of the kitchen made me want to scream. There were dirty pots and pans everywhere. Plates, napkins, silverware covered the counters and stove. As for the halls, living room, and porch, plastic wine glasses and beer bottles vied with cocktail napkins to distribute litter everywhere, including Corinthian Lane. I love my neighbors as myself, so after serving breakfast (as well as possible under the circumstances) I picked up as much as I could. At least I got rid of the aluminum beer cans rolling down the street in the gentle morning breeze.

Reggie came, took away the pots, and left me a bill. I thanked him profusely: he really had turned the look of the yard completely around, and thoughtfully stayed within the small budget I'd suggested.

Last, Sally arrived to clean up the kitchen and remove her stuff. She was very generous with me: I got some great salads, pasta, and an amazing chicken dish. She'd made it all herself. I was deeply impressed, even while wishing every vestige of her presence would suddenly vanish. I couldn't fault her for not having everything shipshape—as mother of the groom she was part of the wedding party, after all, and had a luncheon, wedding, and reception that day. Anyhow, she got a lot accomplished that morning, and I was able to work around what was left and fix breakfast the next day.

The wedding guests left, with many hugs and two-sided air kisses. They really were sweet, and I'd enjoyed meeting them. One deeply puzzling fact, though: the two twin top sheets in Amidships vanished during that weekend and haven't been seen since. I am quite sure the mother and daughter who stayed there would have had zero interest in my off-white cotton sheets. The mystery remains unsolved.

The rental company arrived, dismantled the tables and piled up the tablecloths to go to the laundry. They promised no sheets were involved.

Eventually, of course, it all finally did vanish. When Toby arrived the following weekend, many trips to the dump and adjoining recycle area (by me) had cleared kitchen and basement, and the house had begun to right itself. I myself was not so quick to recover. I was tired and discouraged. The worst was that I had had an awful time, worked like crazy, and hadn't even charged the Greeks and Argentinians, who it turned out were paying the bill, half enough. I had thought Sally was paying and was giving her, as a single mother, a break. The guests were clearly rich and delighted to throw it around: I could have charged six times what I had. How dumb.

After explaining this to Toby, I said, "I'm not a very good business-woman." I twirled my wine glass gloomily around by the stem.

"Come on, sweetie. You've made enough to cover your ginormous property tax, Ben's work, and a whole lot more," Toby observed. "A bad businesswoman couldn't have done that."

"Thanks for being such a support, but I feel as though someone else would've been sure to get real money for that rehearsal dinner. I worked so unbelievably hard, particularly afterwards, and I've got next to nothing to show for it. And I'm so tired. And the wedding guests didn't like sharing their bathrooms!"

"Let's go to a movie," said Toby.

Getting out of the house turned out to be a good idea, and the next several days passed pleasantly. But when he went back home, I began to think very hard about what I was doing and whether or not I was cut out for running a B & B.

It looked as though, after more than three years of running Marble-head on Harbor, I had, rather than settling into the job, begun to feel worse about myself as a proprietor. I was terribly concerned about the physical plant—not a hair or speck of dust anywhere, fresh cookies every after-noon, and a comprehensive buffet each morning, usually with something homemade. And yet as hard as I worked, I was constantly scared I wouldn't measure up: I felt there were a multitude of Barbaras out there, waiting to send damaging reviews about the place and me to TripAdvisor. The threat felt real and very close, although speaking in numbers, it truly wasn't.

And that was only part of the problem. The other huge worry was that I'd forget a guest or double-book a room. Catherine, Mitchell Beal, and Tovar could attest that this had happened. When it had happened, actu-ally, these people had been remarkably decent about it. But the guilt over spoiling someone's trip, or putting a hiccup in it, weighed very heavily on me, and a resulting sense of failure dogged my days. I even worried that I might be in the early stages of some kind of dementia. Why was it so hard for me to write down dates after a conversation or email message? Maybe I was just getting stupid. Maybe that's what dementia was—just a more intense form of stupidity.

When November first finally came around, all the versions of Frankenstein's monster, the vampires, and the witches had disappeared from Salem, and the city was navigable again, I made the decision to close the B & B and move on to the next stage of my life.

This wasn't done without soul-searching and sincere regret. I had loved virtually all the people I'd met; I'd enjoyed sharing my house and my best stuff; I'd been thrilled when things went well; and I'd loved the money. Financial worries are never pleasant, and I'd been mugged by Larry's illness. But all these pluses couldn't counter the frightened feeling in the pit of my stomach that now rarely left me.

I told Toby: he was delighted. I was glad, as I really hoped to have him spend more time at my house, especially in the summer, when it shows to best advantage. I told my children, somewhat shamefaced, as they had given me so much help and encouragement and spent so many hours helping me make it work. But they were happy for me, and pointed out that I'd made enough money so I'd not had to invade the principal quietly growing in my portfolio; and the house was in better shape than it had been for years. The money worries were, by and large, over. And surely, they both said, I ought to feel good about myself for making a success of it. All this was gratifying. But there was more.

One Sunday night Toby and I came home to a dark house. We'd spent the afternoon with Ann and Dudley attending a craft fair. A craft fair! I hate craft fairs and I thought they did too. I couldn't quite fathom it, but it's always fun to be with them and they gave us a big glass of wine at the Boston Yacht Club, where the fair was happening, which helped a lot. When we opened the door of MoH, 40 people jumped out of the darkness shouting, "Surprise!" The children had invited basically my local email address book to a party billed as Operation Mumzi Freedom. Toby and the Welches were of course in on the surprise and had spent the afternoon keeping me away from the house. The party was wonderful, with many people I hadn't seen for so long. I realized how very much I loved having my home back again and being able to entertain my friends the way I wanted to.

I also had a great sense of accomplishment. I had done what I'd meant to do. I had seen Larry through his illness, been with him through some awful times, and stuck with him. With Ben's help, I'd transformed the house from the home of a semi-invalid and nurse—I'd let it get into a mess when waiting on Larry had seemed (and was) more important—to a viable B & B. I was very proud of it. And with the bed and breakfast I'd managed to repair our fortunes and felt secure in my financial situation. Despite my mistakes, I even felt proud of myself.

Self promoting.
needy for positive attention. That she
p. 134         never received from
her mother (and
her father.)

# PART THREE

# CHAPTER 22

Winter came, and so did Toby, who said it was really, really quiet in Barnstable. Marblehead is quiet in the winter also, with many people heading
for Florida. But we had each other, and it was cozy. Despite Paris and its
disappointments, I was still crazy about him.

Toby was super talented musically and sang in two choral groups in
Barnstable. A former piano player, he'd always been interested in the cello,
loved the sound, loved the works written for the instrument. So for Christmas I gave him cello lessons and rented him a cello. I watched him play
and smiled. One day as I walked into the room I heard him say under his
breath:

"Best Christmas present *ever.*"

As I mentioned, we loved a lot of the same music. Not just the oldies
from the sixties, but sacred choral music, Bach and Handel, symphonies,
even opera, though that was more to my taste than his. One night Toby
read that his favorite folk singer was coming to Marblehead the end of
January. I read further and discovered *my* favorite folk singer was sharing
the stage with him! Destiny, for sure. We went and had a fabulous time.

Before we'd met, I'd begun taking voice lessons: I loved the teacher,
who quickly understood what I wanted most was to sing opera arias and
anything at all by Purcell and Handel. We had a delightful session each
week. At least I did. They may have had to tie her up after an hour of me.

One day after I'd been practicing in the living room with the door
closed, I gave Toby a hug and said lightly, "Listen: please tell me if you hear
me doing something right."

"I will," he said.

"Wait! Does this mean I haven't done anything right yet?" I felt deflated.

"Well…you're learning." My feelings were hurt. Clearly I was even worse than I thought.

Toby went back down to Barnstable in February. Everything was fine, he said when he called, except that something was wrong with the heating system and it would take a while to fix so he would have to stick around. In the meantime, he got an exciting call.

"They want me to come back and coach girls' crew from March through May!" he told me. This would be at the school where he'd taught and coached.

"How terrific! Will you live at the school?"

"Possibly I could, but I have a better idea. Why don't we rent an apartment close to the lake, and we can both live there?"

It sounded wonderful. Without the B & B, I had as yet no serious commitments. And I was writing a children's story that I thought had some potential. In another life, I had written several books about grammar and vocabulary that had found publishers: this was a change of pace. I could sit wherever we lived and write on my laptop to my heart's content. Best of all, I would be with Toby.

We went scouting and, after some dead ends, found an apartment we both liked. We scavenged a dining room table, four chairs, and a bed from Toby's daughter; and a bunch of living room furniture and two bureaus from my basement (mostly my mother's stuff). I brought flatware and cooking tools from the house, where I had duplicates of just about everything. We actually *bought* a shower curtain and a tub mat. That just about did it—amazing how easy it can be to set up a new dwelling place. Toby's Sarah was even kind enough to come over and arrange the furniture for us. It took her about ten minutes to tell us what to do. And it was perfect.

"Is this a skill you inherited from your mother?" I quizzed her.

"She definitely didn't get it from me," said Toby.

I was lost in admiration—no way could I have figured out the ideal configuration of sofa, chairs, and dining room table. I revised my estimate of Toby's wife a little. Some good genes there.

The apartment complex was just about four miles from the lake where Toby's girl crews would do their thing. There was a laundry room in the basement and an exercise room in the building next door. The latter was exciting for me: I took breaks from the writing and rode the bike, walked the treadmill, jumped up and down on the elliptical trainer. I felt wonderful about myself: I was exercising my brain with the writing and my body at the little gym. And of course, the most marvelous part of all, I was actually living with Toby—not in my house or his, but in a lovely neutral space that made our commitment seem somehow more official.

I had begun to realize that we might not get married, both being already wedded as we were to our respective houses. And I had seen that he had his flaws like everyone else. He had behaved in some odd and unworthy ways. His weight was unchanged, and he ate a lot and drank what seemed like a lot to me, as I carried bottles to the recycle. I told him the number of bottles was worrying me. He said he slept poorly and would get up in the night and have a drink or two to help him sleep. I don't think it works that way, but I didn't challenge him.

I loved him fiercely, and was happy to do his laundry, keep house, help fix meals, and take out the questionable recycle. Just to be with him, I guess. No fool like an old lady, as they say. In return I received incredibly sweet, affectionate texts throughout the day:

"Dear Sweetie, I'm on my way home. Can't wait to see you! Can I pick up anything for dinner at the store? Love you so much."

I inhaled these messages greedily. He loved me so much!

Even if we never got married, we could work something out. I felt as though we were indeed committed to one another.

And as if this weren't enough, Toby suggested I might want to come to Barnstable in June for the summer, when the crew coaching ended. I was dazed with joy. I could live with him the whole summer!

Of course, I'd be missing summer in Marblehead, which is really hard to top, but it would also give me another opportunity to bring in some income: if I wasn't going to be using the house, why not rent it out? In the summer, Marblehead rentals go for big bucks. I told my friend Anne.

"You should talk to the Hoffmans," she said, referring to a family we knew who'd retired and moved to Florida. "Sue told me they're looking for a place to rent for several months for themselves and their family."

It seemed heaven sent: the Hoffmans were thrilled, I was thrilled. Parents, children, and grandchildren would be coming and going in and out while they were there. Using the beloved house while I was away. This really meant a lot to me.

I made the trip to Marblehead to put away some things that would probably be in their way or get broken by grandchildren. Emptying closets and drawers was little problem, as I had done that when I started the B & B and hadn't yet refilled them with my clothes. With Charlie's help, I cleared large chunks of kitchen shelfage. Charlie emptied out the refrigerator. We bought soap, dishwashing liquid, Cascade for the dishwasher, even a few new washcloths. He nailed the trash chute in the kitchen shut, lest some small child should decide to explore and land one flight down in a garbage can.

Of course Charlie also had to draft the rental agreement, which somehow he knew how to do. (Let the record show that a year later, when Charlie unexpectedly got into debt, I took care of it. I never could have managed the house, B & B years, or rental, without him.) When the Hoffmans arrived I came to Marblehead again, they signed, I signed, and we were in business. I would be making almost as much money (always an issue dear to my heart, though I was pretty happy with my finances now) as I had with MoH, with much less work. Toby wondered if he should get some of the money; I pointed out I hadn't charged him rent to live with me in the winter months. I was mildly astonished he'd even think of it.

So for three months, Toby went to the lake each day and put his girls through their paces. And each day I worked on my children's book and walked and worked out and even did some light housework and cooking.

The last day in the apartment was also the last day of crew: Toby came back with two amazing presents from the girls. There was a beautiful framed and signed photograph of all of them with him. But best of all, they had made a poster that everyone signed, with message so sweet and sincere and frankly adoring that both of us shed a few tears.

"You have to feel this was worth it," I said.

"Even as hard as I had to work." Toby had told me that after seven years off the job, getting back into crew coaching was difficult for him.

The move to Barnstable was complex: we needed to return Sarah's furniture to her basement; return my things to my basement; and put Toby's and my clothes and other gear into his car to take to Barnstable. I followed the moving van to Concord, then to Marblehead, supervising the unloading of stuff. I took a final tour of 15 Corinthian Lane to make sure everything was in place for the Hoffmans' arrival.

"I'll miss you, house—I'll miss you a lot, but I'll be back in October. Be good to the Hoffmans."

I headed down to Barnstable joyfully. Toby welcomed me and helped me get my things upstairs.

"Put your clothes in this closet. I've cleared out this bureau for you. Do you need any help? We have a roast chicken for dinner."

"I need some flowering plants for the deck," Toby said. "And I'd like to buy some tomato plants. Do you want to come to the nursery with me?"

Off we went, collected a number of plants and brought them home. We repotted the three tomato plants in big pots with improved soil and were delighted with our efforts. I stuck my hands in my pockets with pardonable pride. Amazed, I pulled out a wad of cash I'd totally forgotten a guest had given me awhile back.

Did I mention it was a great pleasure for me to spoil Toby?

"You and I are going to the best restaurant on the Cape—my treat!" I said. We went to a French restaurant, where Toby ordered the foie gras as an appetizer. I remember it because I'm not that into it. I had escargots. We both had some fabulous cut of beef. Toby had a gorgeous soufflé for dessert: I was too full to order anything. We rolled home, sleepy and happy.

# CHAPTER 23

I hadn't realized this in Marblehead, where I set the pace, but it was obvious as the days went by in Barnstable that Toby was quite sedentary: his greatest pleasure seemed to be watching television. We watched a lot of soccer. I wasn't used to much television, and Larry had disdained any sport in which he wasn't personally participating. This was new, and a guilty pleasure.

Then I got restless. Actually, spectator sports aren't so much my thing either, and it looked as though Toby himself was asleep part of the time. One afternoon I decided the yard needed some attention and went out with a rake and a few garbage bags. It looked so much better after I'd gotten the two or three years' worth of leaves off the lawn that I felt good. Also I was sure it had burned a lot of calories. When I proudly showed my work to Toby, he just stared. Sort of disappointing.

The third week I was in Barnstable, Toby had some bad sleep problems. Nothing seemed to help. He was afraid making love would make it worse.

"Sweetie, would you mind if I asked you to sleep in the guest room?"

"Of course not—I'll probably sleep better too. I won't be disturbing you if I have to get up."

The next day he told me with a broad smile, "I slept better than I have in weeks."

Ouch. I was happy for him, but that hurt a little: He slept better without me. You could easily make the jump to He doesn't want me in his bed. I brushed the thought aside.

That afternoon we went to the Dennis Playhouse for the matinee performance of "Kiss Me, Kate," a musical I've loved for years. At the end there's a song I think is kind of unexciting, about women and their lot. Bored, I looked over at Toby and saw to my amazement that he was crying. After the show, which is truly not sad, I asked him why. He replied that he was feeling sad about what women have to endure. That didn't sound like him, and I didn't really believe it was true. What was the crying actually about?

That night I slept in the guest room again. Toby, after kissing me good night, said archly, from the door: "And the one who wakes up first gets to wake the other one!" The meaning seemed clear.

The next morning I woke up early but stayed in bed: I wanted Toby to wake me. I waited for almost an hour. He finally stuck his head in the door.

"Time to get up! I'm going down to fix breakfast." This was not at all what he'd hinted at last night. I realized we hadn't made love for maybe a week.

"Toby, what's the matter? Come get in bed with me."

He climbed into bed fully dressed, shut his eyes, and folded his hands over his chest.

"What are you doing? Are you upset with me over something? What's wrong?"

"I think I need some time—and some space." He kept his eyes shut tight.

"That's okay," I said, though I was hurt. "I have to go to Marblehead tomorrow anyhow: I'll stay through the weekend and next week. That next weekend I have a party to go to at the Corinthian and a book club meeting. That'll give you ten days for yourself. I'll stay with Allie or Anne, or maybe Sarah and John." My daughter Sarah and her husband John were celebrating their tenth wedding anniversary at Hawthorne by the Sea, and I was looking forward to attending the event.

I was outwardly nice about Toby's behavior, but I was truly upset. This seemed to have come out of the blue. Why? I'd thought we were happy. Obviously, he wasn't. However, this was the longest time I'd stayed in *his* house. I figured it probably was an adjustment for him after living alone down here for eight or nine years. He'd have some time alone and be glad to see me when I got back. We could talk then.

I spent the day collecting the things I'd need for Sarah and John's party and for the book club, which featured not just the usual ten to fourteen women, but their significant others. I'd hoped to talk Toby into coming to it with me—we were reading a book about Germany's sabotaging behavior before America got into World War I. I was sure it would interest him—but he was a slow reader and had paid little attention to my invitation.

"Aren't you coming to the reception for Principessa Marconi?" he asked. As a trustee of the Marconi Museum in Chatham, he was expected to be there. (Little-known fact: Guglielmo Marconi, inventor of the wireless, chose Mussolini as the best man in his wedding. I didn't stress this to Toby, for whom Marconi was a hero because of the radio thing.) Astonished again, I answered, "Of course: I can leave straight from the museum for Sarah and John's party." I'd thought he wanted time and space ASAP. But maybe he was expected to bring a date.

The next day was cloudy and gray, a good match for my mood. I loaded the car. Toby was behaving oddly: he kept running to the car with items he thought I'd forgotten.

"Here's your prayer book and hymnal. You don't want to leave that behind! And here are your binoculars. Here, take them."

It was as if he was trying to sweep every trace of me out of his house. I could hardly believe it. Also it made no sense: most of my clothes and belongings were upstairs in his closet and bureau. He seemed almost crazy; he was also hyperemotional and kept tearing up again. What on earth?

That afternoon, I followed his car to the museum. I was wearing a dress I'd bought the previous fall to go to the wedding of Toby's nephew. It was a truly beautiful black and metallic copper masterpiece, and I looked as good as I've ever looked: in fact, not too bad for a 69-year-old. We met the Principessa Maria Elettra, Marconi's daughter, an attractive, energetic woman in her 80s. I grabbed some wine and a few hors d'oeuvres and said my goodbyes.

"I'll call you tonight," Toby said.

"Don't do that. Give yourself the full benefit of the time off." And I set off for Swampscott.

The anniversary party was lovely; I couldn't help enjoying it, seeing how pretty and happy Sarah looked, and what a genial host John was. Then I bunked in at Allie's in Swampscott and tried to get some sleep. This didn't go well: I kept tossing and turning and wondering whether I had done something awful; whether Toby had met someone new (How? Where?); whether I had been clingy (I really hadn't); whether, by doing a few good works around the house, I had made him think I was trying to move in permanently (I didn't think so); whether, by suggesting that he eat and drink less, I had seemed like a nag. One night, I remembered, I had smelled something burning and raced downstairs—to find Toby eating an entire package of wild rice out of the saucepan with a big cooking spoon. Perhaps I had embarrassed him.

"I was hungry," was all he said by way of explanation. He sounded as if I'd hurt his feelings.

The next morning, exhausted, I dragged myself to Marblehead to spend the weekend with Anne. She gave me some Ambien at bedtime, which knocked me right out, and the next morning told me some bad stories about her husband and husbands in general, which was really very helpful. But I still felt sad.

Eventually, I moved over to Sarah's, feeling I was imposing on Anne, though she was wonderfully cordial. Sarah and John didn't ask many questions, and it was good to be with the children, now nine and seven.

On Wednesday the hammer fell. I was driving, and I pulled over when I saw a text message from Toby. What I saw froze me to the bone. The message said that he felt he needed to live alone; that he had just "run out of gas;" that he was sorry.

I think he said he was sorry.

I stared at the phone in disbelief. Though I'd had warnings the previous week, I simply couldn't get my head around it. I'd thought we were so close. I'd thought we were happy. Well, *I'd* sure been happy. Where had this come from?

And a few minutes after I'd absorbed the shock, Who breaks up with someone via text? How cowardly! How tacky! How immature! I had thought at least we'd talk things over together.

I called Elaine and drove to Newton, tears blinding me. She was terrific. She took me to the new Wegman's supermarket, where she admired the heaps of shrimp and pyramids of green peppers and I felt as though a deep, physical darkness was closing in on me. Then we went to the movie "Jersey Boys," which was a great call: I love all Frankie Vallee's songs. I love to hear men sing like women: let's not even ask why. Then we went to Elaine's, where I sobbed my way through the night.

At breakfast Elaine said, "How bad is it? Do you wish you two had never reconnected?"

"Yes! Actually, I wish he'd never been born."

"That's bad."

I drove home and called my forever therapist Gina. She asked if I could meet her at the cemetery in Marblehead, a beautiful place, where I sobbed some more and she called Toby many bad names, the kindest of which was sociopath. Her thought was that Toby was somehow a stand-in for the mother and father I'd always tried so hard to please, that I felt *right* when I was with him because I knew they had really approved of him. (In fact, I believe he was the *only* person they ever approved of.) Gina's observations were helpful. But I was still heartbroken.

Because, as Gina said, I had felt so incredibly right in the relationship with Toby, the pain of loss was acute and hard to shake off. But I began to realize, bit by bit, that I'd carried the bulk of that relationship. No pun intended. And that Toby was far from perfect.

There is something my friend Adelaide told me once: people who have lived much or most of their lives in boarding school, in some important ways may not ever really grow up. A lot has been done for them—they've perhaps been given a car to drive, someone services it for them, someone fixes appliances and paints the rooms when they're dingy, etc., and they remain a little bit like grown-up children. (Toby's match.com nickname, "Such a Good Boy," in retrospect makes him sound very much like a grown-up child.) Also, because they make relatively little money, they feel entitled to whatever they can get their hands on. Adelaide lived in a boarding school for thirteen years, while her husband was headmaster, and I think she has it right.

Examples: Toby and I went on a lovely trip with four friends: we all put money into a kitty and Toby was in charge of it. The kitty disappeared from the car, never to be seen again. Where could it possibly have gone? Therapist Gina was certain Toby had just pocketed the money. I found this oddly comforting. It seemed to go with cheating the currency lady at Logan.

As for the grown-up child issue, breaking up with someone you've invited to live with you rates high on the list of self-centered, juvenile behaviors—especially when you know she can't get back into her house for three months. And when you know how much she loves the house and how much of a consolation it would be to get back to it. I was beginning to think I was better off out of that relationship. Why had I not seen it before? Even though the yearning for Toby, unreasonable as it was, was still powerful with me.

And on his side, perhaps I hadn't picked up on how reclusive he was: how he longed for solitude and quiet, and how very much time we had spent together. Was it just too much for him? And yet it seemed as though he'd been the driving force in putting us together so long: starting with his sojourns in Marblehead, then the invitation to the apartment while he coached, and finally to Barnstable. All of this had been his idea—not that I hadn't been overjoyed. And right up to the end he'd been so sweet, so loving. Had he just suddenly snapped? Was he afraid I would try to force him to move to Marblehead? To get married?

I went to my usual book club get-together, where I admired the spouses and significant others. Actually, there weren't that many of the latter. If anyone asked about Toby, I told them the truth, and was greeted with lots of sympathy and suggestions that clearly something was wrong with him— a sentiment that cheered me up. And I enjoyed dinner and the discussion of Germany's efforts to undermine the United States before the Great War.

Toby's hurling me out of his house left another problem to be solved: where on earth was I going to live for three months? How could he have done something so callous and self-centered? The Hoffmans were living in my house, as he knew perfectly well. Several very lovely people offered their houses, one out in beautiful Lenox that my kind friend Bonnie wasn't living in except for weekends here and there. But I was still feeling enough heartache that I didn't want to be with anyone but my own family.

# CHAPTER 24

Of course the logical choice when you are homeless is to call on your family. They're the ones who have to take you in. At least I hoped so. Hat in hand I went to Sarah and John's and begged them to house me for the rest of my exile from home. They were wonderful: they gave me their entire third floor for my own. I was and still am unbelievably grateful. And they sweetly told me they had always hated Toby: they'd found him unappreciative, entitled, and boorish.

I thought this was a little strong, though again it was nice of them. He obviously had faults, that much was becoming clear. Had I been somehow hypnotized into believing he was many things that he wasn't? Or made him up, the way I wanted him to be? Had I hypnotized myself?

The grandchildren were loud in their condemnation, though their biggest gripe, naturally, was his girth. I'd tried to do something about that, longing to see the beautiful, lithe young man I was sure was still in there somewhere—but I'd gotten nowhere. Maybe that's where I'd gone wrong: maybe I'd tried too hard to fix him. When you're nearly 70, maybe you don't want to be fixed. I myself don't want to be fixed, so it stands to reason.

I called Connie, seeking still more sympathy.

"I don't think you're missing much," she said. "I really don't think Toby is all that smart. Pleasant, but not very smart."

Of course that's what she used to say about my various boyfriends when we were in college, but it was still comforting. The problem actually is that Connie and her husband Harold are both so smart they could probably recreate civilization if a nuclear event laid waste the earth. So they think most people aren't smart.

Connie went on: "Re: Toby, by the way, Harold says that when a man rejects a beautiful, intelligent, and devoted woman, you have to suspect depression."

This was the best of all! Beautiful! Intelligent! Harold never says anything that nice to me, or about me. And since he has a Nobel Prize in medicine, I was convinced that his guess about Toby was a good one. (And that his taste in women is unerring.)

At any rate, I lay on the beautiful white bedspread in Sarah's third floor, looked out on a glorious ocean view, and cried till I couldn't see. Lying on my back, I let the tears trickle into my ears. I made lists of Toby's faults. I called other friends for validation: Was I a bad person? I read and reread his emails and his texts, so loving and charming, right up to the end.

"Dearest Becky, This afternoon with you was the most wondrous thing I have ever experienced." I quote. How thrilled I had been to receive that message! And such a short time after that, this unspeakable misery. What the hell had happened?

I wondered whether he was faking the whole time. I wondered whether someone else had burst into his life and upended ours. One of his girls on the crew? Kind of creepy. I wondered whether he was gay. Or experiencing a spiritual crisis. Or depressed, as Harold had suggested. It actually made the most sense. But it really didn't matter: he was gone, and I was alone. I cried some more.

After lying there for about a week in June, I decided I could at least lift my spirits with exercise. John has installed a very nice gym on the third floor. I ran on the treadmill, rode the bike, stomped rhythmically on the elliptical trainer. I tried not to think about how happy I'd been in the spring, doing these very exercises in Toby's and my apartment complex. I trooped around the neighborhood: I soon knew almost every street in Swampscott, not to mention everyone who walks a dog. And I swam in the ocean as if I were drowning: back and forth, back and forth until I was exhausted. I sat in the sun with the water beside me and tried to read, but I couldn't concentrate.

I heard that my friend Jane had hollered across the yacht club tennis court: "Hey! Did you hear Becky got dumped?"

When this was repeated to me, I said,

"Excellent! There are five courts within earshot, with four women on each court. Surely one of those 20 women has a single brother or cousin who wants to meet me."

But I didn't mean it. How could I ever feel about anyone as I'd felt about Toby?

People were lovely: they invited me out for many lunches and dinners. Jean, probably the kindest woman in all of Marblehead, who never says a cross word about anyone, stepped outside herself for this one, giving vent to some serious fury regarding Toby and his behavior. I was touched. Seven-year-old Eliza Westwood even asked me, by written invitation, to a tea party in her bedroom. Children are empathetic little creatures, and my broken heart was warmed by her kindness. But nothing could really fix the pain I felt inside. At some level, I realized he wasn't worth it, but that was an intellectual realization. My love for him was purely emotional.

I emailed Toby that we needed to meet: I had a lot of stuff belonging to him from the apartment, and of course he had just about all of my clothes. He called, and we arranged to meet more or less halfway at a McDonald's in Plymouth the following week. I am ashamed to say I looked forward to seeing him—just seeing him, just talking to him.

When I got to McDonald's he was there. I saw him before he saw me. I just looked at him, thinking how truly unattractive he was, and how desperately I cared for him. We sat down for a Coke and to share news. He was on the verge of tears several times. Something was going on with him and it wasn't just me. We exchanged possessions and hugged goodbye. He began to cry.

"Stop it or you'll have me in tears too," I told him severely. I drove out of the parking lot with a heavy heart. As long as he'd had my clothes, I knew I'd see him again. Now it was really and truly over.

I got back, dragged myself up to the third floor, and burst into tears. Fast becoming my default setting. Nothing, I felt, could compensate me for losing this person. And yet I knew that, rationally speaking, I hadn't lost much worth keeping.

As June gave way to July, which dragged on into August, I began to feel I should get out of the Westwoods' hair. John travels a lot for work, and when he's home, he likes to be king of the castle, and I don't blame him. I tried to make myself scarce, but I didn't always succeed. On one memorable night, at 10:30, I locked him out. I felt terrible. I needed to minimize the time I was there.

Ann and Dudley, God bless them, invited Elaine and me to cruise with them for a long week. Elaine shook up daiquiris, Ann fixed fantastic meals, and Dudley guided us around Rhode Island. We had two kayaks that saw a lot of use. We had fantastic weather, and the scenery was beautiful. Dudley said he wouldn't ever have had Toby on the boat for more than a few hours—he hinted that he was afraid the deck would collapse or the boat would sink. This was consoling.

And then, as luck would have it, my next-door neighbors on Corinthian Lane needed someone to feed their rabbit and water their tomatoes while they were away for ten days. Of course I would! I moved in in late July and had the interesting experience of waking up to see my house right across the way, filled with kids and grandchildren. Apart from having some trouble working the coffee machine, the Hoffmans were doing fine. And each day when I got up, my house looked more beautiful, shiny white in the morning sun. How much I loved it!

I felt bad about the house. For someone who had protested so strongly that she would never willingly leave it, nor consign it to the wrecking ball, I had certainly taken off blithely when Toby whistled. In fact, I'd abandoned it for almost five months. Now once again, it seemed unbelievably precious to me. But it belonged to the Hoffmans for another month and a half.

I emailed Connie:

*When I think about it I could kick myself. I was in love—in fact, absolutely besotted—with a person I believed was good, and kind, and trustworthy. He wasn't. Now I'm homeless. This really isn't much fun. And I'm house-sitting right next door to my own wonderful house. Which I miss like crazy. Much love XXOO*

Connie emailed back:

*I told you he wasn't very smart. This is the kind of thing not-smart people do. Also, you told me Adelaide said these lifer boarding school types often don't quite grow up. This is the kind of self-centered, teenager-ish behavior one might expect from a 17-year-old, yes? He is utterly unworthy of you so do yourself a favor and forget him. Much love.*

Connie is a dear friend but definitely given to tough love. Pull up your socks!

I wrote:

*Easy for you to say. Love in the later years seems to hang on—maybe because we aren't sure we can find someone else to love? But it's more than that. I gave Toby my heart and soul and he's trashed them both. You can't imagine the pain. Much love. XXOO*

She replied:

*Tell him to give them back. I frankly think you need a change of scene: come visit us in September. We're in the Berkshires the whole month with not so many plans, and it would be a treat to see you—assuming you've dried your tears at least somewhat. Harold hasn't any patience with tears. Much love.*

She usually has good ideas and this was one. I was on the same wavelength. While I was house-sitting, I began to incubate a plan—an excellent opportunity to give the Westwoods some space and myself some new vistas. I'd always wanted to go out west, particularly after seeing Ken Burns's special on the National Parks. (Toby had had zero interest. He'd seen them when he was twelve or something. Please.) Charlie came to the rescue again: he had a credit card that gave him concierge services and he got the concierge to make plane and lodge reservations and book a rental car for me! This was fantastic.

Several kind ladies offered to come on the trip with me, but I wanted to be by myself. Actually, I wondered, having spent many years traveling with someone else, whether I *could* be by myself. Whether, in fact, I could cope with practical matters as men and many women do. I had never, for example, picked up a rental car alone or checked into a hotel. As for finding my way around, I have never been one bit of good at that. Would I be able to find Zion and Bryce canyons and get back to my lodge? We were going to see.

It turned out to be a super trip. I managed to get from the airport to the rental car kiosk, dodge round a flash flood via GPS, and arrive at the lodge where Charlie's concierge had booked a little cabin that was all mine. Each morning after breakfast, I sat on the porch, drank a second cup of coffee, and watched the sun rise and light up the sheer purple and red rock cliffs of Zion. I hiked up many of the trails—and of all things, ran into my Wellesley College classmate Alice and her husband. This made me feel very much at home.

I drove through a blacker-than-night tunnel and round many dreadful and daunting switchbacks to get to Bryce. After I established with a Park

Ranger that if I drove an extra sixty miles back to Zion I could avoid the tunnel and most of the scary roads, I fell in love with the legions of orange hoodoos in the huge amphitheater at Bryce. Hoodoos are those rock formations that look amazingly like people, often people with pots on their heads. I clambered down into the amphitheater via several trails. It was exhausting, and beautiful, and fun. You look up at the Zion cliffs and trails, but down at Bryce. It made for an interesting pair of parks to visit.

Later, people asked me whether I'd been frightened hiking alone. The answer is that I was rarely even close to alone. There were always people just in front of me and just behind me, and if I'd ever felt uncomfortable, it would've been easy just to say, May I walk with you for a bit? The people hiking in those canyons seemed uniformly friendly and well-intentioned.

I won't deny that a bit of my pleasure on this trip came from sending Toby a postcard showing some monster cliffs and saying: "As you know, this is something I've been longing to do. Having a terrific time."

But I was definitely not the same heartbroken woman I'd been two months before. I was feeling better. Zion and Bryce had done some excellent work.

I went on to Seattle, where I visited my Wellesley friend Diane and her family, ate huge shrimp and homemade ice cream and saw Steller's Jays at her birdfeeders—beautiful birds with black heads and crests and gorgeous royal blue feathers. Diane was terrific: it was obvious she didn't want to talk about Toby and she refused to let me do it: she cut me right off when I tried. This was also good for me. Visiting Diane, her husband Ray, and their daughter Sarah was altogether a healing experience.

I arrived back at Sarah and John's feeling invigorated and much more positive. The image of Toby as a lover had faded greatly: I didn't feel a pang if I thought of his face, or any other part of him. I had stopped crooning over things we had done or bought together—the hair dryer Toby ordered! Cattails! That afternoon at the museum! These things no longer had the power to break my heart; I could face them and still feel pretty good. I'd even come to realize that, except when the morning sun flooded the front rooms, his house was dark. Like, very dark. And loaded up with a hodge-podge of indifferent and uninspiring furniture that looked like stuff scavenged from a parental downsizing. Which it probably was.

During my solitary walks on the canyon trails, I had also realized something important. Coincidence is not destiny. Just because both of you have daughters named Sarah with sons named Charlie doesn't make you soulmates. The fact that both of you love the Bach cantata "Wachet auf" best of all doesn't mean you're meant to be together. The fact that you taught Business Writing and he taught French and both of you love words doesn't mean a thing: it's a *coincidence*. And there's nothing magical about it.

Next I went to visit Connie and Harold in the Berkshires.

"I know you've been hiking all over the Southwest, so this hike we're going to take won't faze you," Connie told me.

"Have you considered that all that hiking has worn me to a frazzle?"

"Well, it was probably easier than running Marblehead on Harbor."

The hike turned out to be eight miles long, longer than many trails I'd been walking. I was delighted with myself for being able to keep up: probably all that walking, swimming, and working out in Swampscott had helped as much as the canyon hikes.

Then back to the Westwoods' for just a few days. I packed up and said tearful goodbyes to everyone. I sent them the biggest floral arrangement Salvy the Florist could muster, but nothing will ever be big enough to express my gratitude to them.

I arrived home the day after the Hoffmans left. The house was neat and sparkling and seemed to welcome me back. I'm not ashamed to say I actually threw myself on the floor and kissed the rug in the hall. Dramatic, yes, but it was just the way I felt. I have never, ever, been so happy to be home. *House,* I said, *I missed you so much.* Its sturdy bulk seemed to say, *I missed you too.*

# CHAPTER 25

After the excitement subsided and I had unpacked and sorted out my bills and my life, I emailed Toby, telling him he had caused me a great deal of suffering, not to mention inconvenience, and I thought I deserved to know why. He wrote back immediately that he had been having a very hard time, "harder than you know" (*He'd* had a hard time. Hah!) and would very shortly address the issue. Of course he didn't. I never heard a thing. And that was actually okay.

By this time I was no longer pining by the emailbox, waiting to hear just what reason he might give for putting me through the wringer. I had actually been thinking about how pleasant it had been to meet some men through match.com and do lunch. Who knew? I might even meet someone wonderful. I fired up my match.com profile, sat back, and waited.

I immediately heard from a man I'd dated briefly before I met Toby, saying, Don't I know you from a few years ago? We met for lunch: I was glad to see him, but there wasn't a spark on either of our parts. I waited a while. Then one afternoon, I opened up match and found a picture of my match for the day. A slender, craggy-looking man in white shirtsleeves *Fred* peered out from under shaggy blond (maybe gray) bangs over a pair of reading glasses, looking smart, funny, and maybe just a little grouchy. For some reason the face appealed to me. I read his profile, discovered he was three years older than I, a widower, a Harvard graduate, lived on Cape Ann (not too far away), and was in the medical field. Hm. All but the last sounded pretty okay. The medical field covers a lot of jobs. Maybe he was an orderly. Or a diener (that's a morgue assistant.) Only one way to find out.

I sent an email asking him to take a look at my profile and let me know whether he'd like to meet me. I received a message almost instantly to say he would like very much to meet me. He said he was coming to Marblehead the following Tuesday to play squash at the YMCA. Charming: this had the double advantage of sounding elitist (squash) yet democratic (the Y). He said he was afraid to come into Marblehead as he wasn't good at spatial relations and had once gotten terribly lost in its labyrinth of tiny streets. I laughed at this, but I could relate to it strongly: it had taken me years to learn my way around town. He suggested lunch at the Salem Diner: he'd never eaten there, he wrote, but it looked interesting. What? I was amazed. I would *never* suggest lunch at a place I hadn't ever been to. He was either stupid or grossly overconfident. And a diner? Though this particular diner is a very cute Art Deco replica, so he got points. He'd be finishing squash at 11 and hoped we could meet at 11:15. 11:15? For lunch? Definitely getting weirder; probably an orderly. He signed himself Fred. I wasn't hoping for too much, frankly—but he had done some things right, and the email reflected a sort of Old World courtesy that I liked. I said yes.

The following Tuesday I ate breakfast early and pulled myself together. I was still pretty thin and could tuck a pale blue ribbed turtleneck into my black skirt to my advantage. I wrestled my hair into submission and sallied forth.

I recognized him instantly. He actually looked better than his picture—unlike most people on match. He stood when I came over. Good. He was quite tall. Good. A scholarly stoop. Don't mind that. We shook hands. Sat. Began to talk: he was very easy to talk to and listened amazingly well. When I asked his occupation and he said he was a retired psychiatrist, I realized that listening was what he had been doing for 40 years. It wasn't just my conversational charm.

My father always said psychiatrists are crazy: that's why they get into the field. From then on I was watching carefully for signs of lunacy. Fred seemed pretty normal so far, even given the choice of restaurant and the 11:15 lunch hour.

The place was very busy: Fred suggested we order. I thought the menu looked appealing but Fred commented that he really loved diner food, especially meatloaf, and was disappointed not to find it on the menu. We ordered sandwiches. The waitress brought our order, including a turkey club for Fred, not the Reuben he had ordered. He signaled and called to the waitress, who was alone and serving about 30 Salem State students. Then he checked himself.

"You know, she's being run off her feet, and this sandwich looks perfectly good. I think I'll just eat it."

His stock soared. It was clear from his manner that he wasn't timid about asking for what he'd ordered: he'd just decided to give the waitress a break. We ate and talked some more. At one point he told me he had wanted to meet me because my profile was funny: I had said I loved opera and hoped, when I died, to be reincarnated as a tenor-baritone duet. He laughed at the memory, and I noticed he had a huge gap between his front teeth. Like many Americans, I am the product of years of orthodontistry, and I was shocked to meet someone who had clearly never had any.

He must have noticed my surprise, because he said, "My second wife wanted me to get rid of the gap between my teeth. I don't know why I never did anything about it."

Second wife? We waded in. He had divorced his first wife after 15 years, his second after 15 more. The reasons were complex, but made sense. His *third* wife had died of a heart attack after enduring years of treatment-resistant depression. She'd been gone about a year and a half. He said that when she died, there was very little left to mourn. I understood that for sure. Also the painful irony of being a psychopharmacologist but unable to help her.

He had two sons, both doctors, by his first wife. He and his second wife had adopted a baby girl, now in her early thirties. So, three children and two ex-wives. Hm again. This bore some thinking about. I shelved it for the time being.

Now for some reason neither of us can recall—maybe because he had impressed me and I wanted to impress him—I managed to work into the conversation that I was well acquainted with the winner of a Nobel Prize in medicine. Connie's husband Harold, as I've mentioned, earned said prize a few years back.

"Interesting," said Fred. "My brother's neighbor has a Nobel Prize in medicine."

You know the rest: Connie and Harold have a house on the same street as Fred's brother Richard and his wife Judy, in a tiny town in the Berkshires. What were the odds? We marveled.

More than that. When you meet people, especially online, you really don't know anything about them except what they tell you. And they could be lying, couldn't they? It's different with a blind date (wonder if they even happen anymore?): at least you have a friend/relative in common who has im- or explicitly vouched for the person. The fact that Fred had a brother, married and living in a town and on a road I had visited many times, went a very long way in establishing his bona fides. Well, and it was all I had, and I liked him.

We left the diner and began our goodbyes.

"I'd like to do this again," Fred said.

"Why don't we have lunch in Marblehead?" I said. "I can give you really, really clear directions to my house and we can go find The Landing together."

He agreed. I gave him a chaste kiss on the cheek and we parted.

On the appointed day, at the appointed time, I saw a white car approach Corinthian Lane, slowly, gingerly, then sweep majestically past. Soon the car came slowly back in the opposite direction. Again it went past. I began to laugh. He hadn't been kidding about being directionally challenged. Finally he appeared to have taken in the (very) large Corinthian Lane sign, and crept at a snail's pace down the hill. I ran out onto the porch to make sure he didn't bypass the house.

Like practically all my guests, he was knocked out by the harbor view. A big thank-you, not for the first time, to the Victorian owner who, in defiance of convention, had installed that huge picture window giving on the water. He went on to admire the heavy Victorian furniture, which appears to advantage against the pale pink wall. He also loved the huge, deep moldings, more typical of a year-round house than the summer house it was built to be. I really appreciated his open enthusiasm. As I mentioned, Toby hadn't said a word about the house. Ever. We had lunch at The Landing and more conversation.

"Wait! You were living on the Cape with someone, and he asked you to leave?" Fred was incredulous. "Clearly not a Mensa candidate: nobody with a brain would do that to you. What's wrong with him?"

"I don't know, and I'm starting not to care. He's just somebody that I used to know."

"Because I've got excellent connections to some, ah, interesting people in Gloucester. If you want me to, I can send Tommy Pots and Pans down there to, you know, help him understand that he made a big mistake."

"Thanks, Fred—but I doubt that beating up Toby will solve anything."

"Who da hell knows?" said my smart psychiatrist. He seemed to have a lot of Gloucester in him.

*     a later improvement, perhaps?

When we got back to the house, he put his arms around me and kissed me a kiss that went right down to the soles of my feet. It felt enthusiastic and well practiced. I don't know why this surprised me so much. Though Fred had displayed a sort of diffident charm when we'd met, he certainly should have had some expertise. With all those wives, he must have had plenty of practice. (That's mean. I didn't feel a bit mean towards Fred, and he was still good friends with his living wives, which says something important about him.)

After Christmas I had another date with Fred. I drove up to Gloucester to his condo. Unfortunately, I had lost the email that told me which corner his condo was on and what number was his. I didn't realize this until I got up there. I tried to call him, but I'd also managed somehow to delete his call, so I didn't even have his number. This was awful. I parked the car and considered standing in the middle of the intersection and screaming Fred until he came to his door. Luckily, I picked a good corner and knocked on the door of a woman who knew him.

It got worse. When he opened the door and saw me in my cute dress and fancy shoes, he seemed nonplused. Apparently in the email he had suggested a hike on Ocean Lawn, part of the former Coolidge estate. Sneakers and jeans, yes. Dress and heels, not so much. I explained that I had lost his message, and we took a modified hike—I stumbling along behind. Interestingly, he didn't let me off the hook or give up his plans because of my dumb mistake—then went back to his place, where we had a lovely lunch. I was impressed at his creativity with takeout from Henry's Market in Beverly. We played some of his CDs. I liked his musical choices—maybe a little heavy on the Bach, but smart people seem to like Bach; and he also had some wonderful country and folk and some Appalachian spirituals. We even danced! My idea: I liked being in his arms. And he turned out to be a good dancer.

One problem: he began suggesting that we should "go upstairs." I resisted, because it felt odd. After my unfortunate experience with Toby, I wasn't really ready for a relationship, if that's what we call it nowadays. And we didn't know each other that well. But part of me wanted to oblige.

When I got home, he called. He said, "You know, we could get married."

"Are you out of your mind?"† I answered. This must be what my dad meant. The following week I received a pre-nup agreement in the mail from his lawyer. Definitely crazy. Dating continued.

† yes, he was!

Eventually I gave in to the pleas to go upstairs, which was solidly excellent. Proposals followed. Many proposals. If I visited him, I could hear him on the phone to his brother, his friends, his children, telling them he had found the woman he was going to marry. Well, that was his problem: I wasn't about to marry anyone.

I love opera. Fred said he didn't know much about it but insisted on taking me to the Met simulcasts in Rockport, those movies of operas live from the Met in New York. We watched Verdi, Wagner (too long: Fred insisted on leaving), Puccini, Handel (too long: Fred insisted, etc.). The simulcasts are wonderful. You can see the adorable soprano Anna Netrebko six times life-size.

One night at my house we were cooking dinner while listening to an excellent vintage CD of Maria Callas doing La Traviata, opposite Giuseppe di Stefano as Alfredo. He sings an aria to her, "Un di felice," that captures the beauty of the moment when two people declare their love for one another. I adore it and decided to belt it out for Fred. I turned to face him and began to sing. To my utter amazement, Fred was singing too. In a very nice baritone voice. He even knew the words! I threw myself into his arms, pretty much overcome with emotion.

"You said you didn't know much about opera!" I said.

"I said I didn't know much. I didn't say I was a cave-dweller. And I really love that aria. And you."

"Likewise."

"Marry me. Please."

"No. But thank you." He was quickly becoming very important to me.

In March, we flew to Turks and Caicos, which was heavenly. Clear skies, warm weather, and a very funny companion. We stayed in a small resort one of his friends had recommended, which had a pool and a beach. I had the dubious pleasure of watching Fred snorkel: he put on his mask and one flipper, walked out about 20 feet from the beach, put his face in the water, turned in a circle, and claimed he had seen "lots of fish." When I persuaded him to come out into deeper water, he sank. Luckily, the water was shallow. He seemed surprised, noting that he had a Boy Scout lifesaving badge from his youth. Turns out, says my friend Jennifer, a YMCA swim coach, that as people get older they lose fat and their blood contains less oxygen. No longer buoyant, they tend to sink. Interesting. So much for snorkeling and swimming. Nobody's perfect. I'd had 37 years with a super-athlete, and that would have to do. Actually, there was something refreshing about Fred's different-ness.

A friend's daughter had suggested two restaurants, which we tried and loved. At the second one, we ate in a large red and white dining room filled with big palm trees wrapped in tiny white lights. Fred said plaintively, "Maybe we could have a very long engagement."

"No," I said. "But I appreciate the offer."

After the trip to Turks and Caicos, Fred spent the night more and more often at my house. Sometimes I'd go to Gloucester to his condo. One day when we were at my house, he got up very early, made a trip to the condo, and returned with a Panasonic rice cooker and five pounds of rice.

"Does this mean you're moving in?" I asked. He nodded, busily putting away rice.

He sold his condo in a day, and suddenly we were officially living together. The furniture he had kept fitted in remarkably easily with what was already here: I was thrilled to have another big bookcase in the bedroom, and I got rid of a strange piano-like instrument called a melodeon that made noises like a dying animal when you pushed pedals and tapped keys. I made peace with Fred's very large photograph of three famous baseball players, and Fred was wonderful about the (many) pictures of my late husband and our children.

"Other things being equal, I'd rather live in Gloucester. But you're here, so Marblehead is my home now."

There were a few areas where we didn't agree. Not many, but a few.

"That sofa is really ugly, Becky. In fact, it's hideous."

"It happens to be a Biedermeier piece, and the appraiser said it's worth a lot of money." The object of his distaste was upholstered in tufted brown velvet, and was, to tell the truth, pretty shabby. Probably what the wretched Barbara was referring to.

"Interesting," Fred replied. "That hardly changes the fact that it's nasty to look at."

"Well, I think it's beautiful. And I helped the children carry it up the front steps, so I have a deep sentimental attachment to it."

Fred grumbled, but ultimately let that one pass. About the kitchen carpeting, he was less flexible.

"How long has this been here?"

"Um. About thirty years."

"Time for a change?"

"I love it: you can drop anything on it because it never shows dirt."

"My point exactly." The thought of those years of ground-in dirt unnerved him. The next thing I knew, the indoor-outdoor carpet was gone and a really pretty flooring that looked exactly like wood had been in-stalled—a present from Fred. We each had a couple of Oriental area rugs, which we used to soften the look and give me someplace to drop crockery without breaking it.

*NOT SO!* Fred turned out to be incredibly easy to live with. I found myself thinking he was marvelous, partly because he was good at the words, "You were right," "I'm sorry," and "I was a real jerk last night." Do they teach this in psychiatry school? How wonderful! I had so rarely heard these words from Larry, never from Toby. And because we got along so well, I didn't need to hear them often from Fred. But it was good to know he would admit it if he screwed up.

I should also reference his intellect, his wit, his courtly manners, his sapphire blue bedroom eyes. He had a lovely sense of humor, often self-deprecatory; he would sit motionless for four hours reading a book; and, like my father, when he crossed his legs at the knee, he could almost put the crossing foot on the ground. He was elegant. And unbelievably sweet to me. I became insanely crazy about him (redundant but true).

"Becky, a twenty-something would kill for legs like yours. In fact, for several other body parts. You have the body of a 35-year-old." (A 70-year-old could get used to this kind of talk. In about three minutes.)

Fred, it was quickly clear, was a good bit smarter than I. This also charmed me. I loved watching him tackle a tome on philosophy, politics, or world religions. I couldn't wade through one of those, but I learned a lot from hearing his take on them, and I enjoyed dipping into them myself to get at least the gist.

He could also sing all the verses of the Ode to Joy from Beethoven's Ninth in German. I think most people would love someone who can do that.

I really like to go to church. Our minister delivers a power punch of a sermon, and the organist and choir are brilliant. To my delight, Fred took to the church immediately: he said he loved to sing hymns and enjoyed the sermons as a time for reflection. So each Sunday we went. Afterwards, he would often ask, "Would you like to pay your respects to Larry?" He'd drive up the hill and park, and I'd run down to the Remembrance Garden where many of Larry's ashes are deposited and give him the news of the week.

"Have you ever been to Halibut Point?" A typical Fred intro. "Oh, you've gotta see it—it's beautiful!"

And before I could turn around, we'd be off to Halibut Point, or the Panama Canal, or some place he was sure I would love. Enthusiasm is charming, and it's sexy. Fred was sexy.

No one is perfect, however, and his take on things medical was often catastrophic: I think this is a holdover from second-year med school, where you learn about all the diseases and conditions that can afflict, and sometimes destroy, the human body. Fred seemed to have retained all this knowledge, and every scratch on my arm was going to go septic if I didn't soak it twice a day. I appreciated the TLC but knew it was unnecessary. Eating food that was more than three days old would assuredly give you salmonella or worse. I have been doing this for years: you just scrape off the mold or whatever and enjoy what's left. And if I ever, ever, went into Boston for the evening, I was certain to be attacked by the mother-rapers and father-stabbers lurking on the Blue Line. The Blue Line! Give me a break.

Despite this eccentricity, I found myself falling more and more in love as the weeks turned into months. Or perhaps because of it: Maybe there was something in it that made me feel he cared. No one else has *ever* been worried that I would come to grief on the Blue Line (Prince of Subways).

One morning I woke up and realized I was being truly stupid. Maybe we'd live forever, but I wouldn't bet on it. And I loved Fred very, very much.

"Fred, do you still want us to get married?"

"Of course I do, are you kidding me?"

"If you seriously still want to, I'd be thrilled—I'd be honored— to marry you."

Four months later, in September, we were married at our church in Marblehead.

Fred's two grandsons and my grandson and granddaughter walked down the aisle ahead of me, and Charlie hauled me down to Fred, resplendent in a new suit and shoes. About 100 guests, his friends and mine, filled the church, everyone in a great mood. My music teacher sang one of our favorite Handel arias. It was wonderful.

We had a glorious day, warm but not too warm, with a gentle breeze. My only worry had been that, because it was already September, it would get dark, and I wanted to use the porch. Charlie, ever at hand when trouble struck, had arrived at 11:00 in the morning and nailed strings of lights all around the porch eaves. When night fell it looked magical.

I thought of Sally's rehearsal dinner just a year before: how I had looked through the big picture window at the guests on the porch and felt dispossessed, like a ghost flitting in to furl the flag and then disappearing.

Not any more: I was no longer that sad apparition, taking care of other people in what had once been my castle. I'd taken possession of the porch again and the people on it were our friends and our family once more.

And I hadn't had to sell the house and see it torn down; and we wouldn't until we absolutely had to. And I had salted away enough money to make even me feel secure.

I had loved running Marblehead on Harbor most of the time, and it had in turn been very, very good to me. And I had loved sharing the house with the guests. But it was time for a new chapter.

# APPENDIX

*Pleasing Guests*
*at Marblehead on Harbor*

Hi, Barb:

Thank you for being here! I know you'll make everyone feel wonderful.

Check-in time for guests is 3:00 p.m. or after. I've usually worked this out with them and written their approximate arrival time on their card. I try to be ready earlier than that, as often they are arriving from a distance and can't predict arrival times exactly. If they call and want to come at noon, that is totally your call: I try not to let them do it. Suggest they have a leisurely lunch at the Landing and do some sightseeing.

Before guests arrive, I make sure there is sherry in carafe, two bottles of water (in basement near garage door—three if an extra person in room), a bowl of trail mix, two or three wrapped chocolates, 3 or 4 plastic cups, a couple of cocktail napkins, and two sherry glasses on the tray in each room.

I like to have cookies in the front hall—I'll have a supply of chocolate chip slice 'n' bake available. If you want to get serious with baking, feel free! And maybe a pitcher of water in the dining room. *Crystal Light Lemonade* is on the Lazy Susan to the left of dishwasher if you feel very kind.

You can buy supermarket flowers if there are none in the yard, but pick anything you like: I put just a flower or two in a vase for the room, and an arrangement in the front hall.

When they arrive, I try to help with the suitcases. Usually they insist on taking them up. I show them the living room (be sure to point out the menu book and pamphlets regarding area attractions) and the dining room, where they'll have breakfast. Then I take them to their room and ask if there's anything more they need. Point out that that's sherry in the carafe. Remind them the beach is open to them (if appropriate) and note we have beach towels, which I keep in the corner of the front hall.

I tend not to hang out in the public rooms or on the porch—these are for their use while they are here. If they invite me, I accept enthusiastically.

## LIVING ROOM

There are after-dinner drinks on a tray as you enter the living room. I'm trying to get through all those liqueurs. There are lots of Marblehead and North Shore books on the tables and in the bookcase—guests are welcome to read these in the living room or in their rooms. The piano does not play because it can't be tuned: the pegs and the soundboard are, respectively, metal and wood, and they expand and contract differently. The piano stays in tune 24 hours max. Also, many keys don't play. Everyone's welcome to bang on it, kids included.

## DINING ROOM

Point out the coffee machine: some people drink coffee all day. Put some milk and/or Half & Half in the small refrigerator. And some ice in the freezer. Tell them they can put takeout or whatever in that fridge.

## BEDROOMS

Each bedroom has its own character. Be sure rugs and floor are clean in each (yellow vacuum cleaner is in computer room to the left of the big desk), room dusted, tray with goodies complete, a few flowers in a bud vase on the bureau. Be sure clean sheets and pillowcases are on all the beds. Fluff the dust ruffles. Starboard Home: red pillows on the chaise outdoors if weather is good.

As you know, Amidships can be made up as a king: bedclothes for this arrangement are on the third floor on the lower bunk bed: remember the king-size mattress pad, which makes the whole thing work. Consult your index card to see which configuration they prefer.

## BATHROOMS

I want to be sure the floor is super-clean, so I take a Swiffer wet cloth and zoom over the floor. Then I take a clean Swiffer cloth and wipe down the basin, tub, and toilet (in that order) and swish the toilet bowl with toilet brush. The Swiffer stuff is to the left of the wooden desk in the computer room.

I put a *brand-new* roll of toilet paper on the roller for each new party. Make sure new little wrapped Lord & Mayfair soaps (in cabinet left of the wooden desk near the sliding doors) are in shower and on sink. Check to be sure there's enough shower gel, shampoo, and conditioner in all shower caddies. More of these things are in the cabinet nearest the sliding doors in the computer room. Also check the baskets: is there a disposable razor or two, toothbrush, toothpaste, etc.? More of those are in the same cabinet.

Department of Old Plumbing: It's good to jiggle the handle of the 2nd-floor toilet. Eventually it'll stop—well, usually.

Third-floor bath: I have spent many, many dollars, but the tub drain is still sluggish and we don't know why. I find it's best to mention this ahead of time.

Ask them when they'd like breakfast: my choice is 8:00 a.m.—but most of the time the buffet keeps no matter when they show up. You can nuke anything if they come down late.

If someone requests a key to the room, I have them in a white box on my bureau, labeled for each room. If I hand them out, they get lost. That box also contains a key to the dining room china closet, where you can store anybody's very valuable stuff. Seaview and Steerage have old-style keys in the keyholes or on the bureau. I keep a spare set of the same keys in the top left bureau drawer of my room. And if they'd like the house locked, I give them a house key (on top of the secretary in the front hall) and I lock up when I go to bed, first being sure everybody's in. Remind them to give back the keys!!!

NOTE:
As you probably realize, all the rooms can be locked if you're inside.

When it gets dark, I turn on the outside lights and the front hall light, three switches to the left of the front door as you look out. When everyone is in, I turn them off. If people are late and you've gone to bed, remember to turn them off in the a.m.

BREAKFAST
Check your index cards, where I've noted down any food allergies or special diets. I'll make or buy gluten-free or dairy-free if someone needs it.

Here's my list of things ALWAYS on the buffet or glass cart:

Water
Butter
Jelly
Lemons (sliced, for tea)
Cereals
English muffins (beside toaster)
Bread for toast
Yogurt
Fresh fruit cut up in bowl
Bananas, unopened, beside cereals
Half and half
Milk
Orange juice (once in a while cranberry if long-term guests)

And here are the things I rotate—in other word, perhaps two but not all:

Muffins (made or from shop)
Hard-boiled eggs
Quiche (*Gourmet Shop* on Bessom Street if I don't get to *Market Basket*)
Breakfast bars (recipe over sink)
Zucchini bread (recipe over sink)
Ham
Bacon

Needless to say, you don't have to home-make any of these things! Buy them, charge it to me. Or fix whatever you like: usually on the shelves nearest the back door are ready-to-mix muffins, breads, etc.

I try to hang around if I sense they need guidance regarding places to eat, visit,etc. There should be some maps on the piano to show them how to get to the restaurants and other points of interest. I encourage them to visit the Jeremiah Lee House if it's open, and Abbot Hall, where they can see "The Spirit of '76" and a good version of Leutze's "Washington Crossing the Delaware" (with Marblehead's own Glover's Regiment). There are also lots of pamphlets promoting things to see and do around the region: a man comes every month or so to replenish these, so give them out freely.

If they are here for a specific function, such as wedding or party, of course there's no problem. Remember that they may need directions. Not everybody loves Siri, particularly the elderly.

## CHECKOUT

Checkout time is 11:00 a.m.—I'm reasonable if they can't get out right on time. But it is good to get the bed stripped, the laundry started, and fresh sheets on the bed, because often someone's coming in at 3:00. Or you might get a call from the Chamber of Commerce booth downtown that someone would like to. Sheets for Starboard Home are in the lower drawers of the bureau nearest the sliding doors. For Amidships, they are in the lower drawers of the bureau. For Seaview and Steerage, they're in the blue-green chest in Steerage. You can put any of them on either bed.

## BOOKING ROOMS

I usually handle the email requests from my cell phone, but if someone calls for a room, I'd love it if you'd book them in. Check two things in the folder I'll give you: 1) the index cards, arranged by date; 2) the calendar sheets. If there's nobody in either category, go right ahead.

Remember that Steerage does NOT have its own bathroom but must share with Seaview: I rarely book Steerage unless parents or relatives are going to be in Seaview. I'd lose money if only Steerage is booked, if you see what I mean: I'd much rather book Seaview only, unless someone is clearly trying to economize and you take pity on them.

Note: I find it works best to tell people ahead of time that those two baths, while they are for the use of Seaview/Steerage and Amidships only, are on the staircase landings, because they were built some time after the house (1881). It's a deal-breaker for some people, especially the older folks—also I don't want to mislead or disappoint anyone. I even had one very sincere man who sleeps in the buff change his mind about coming because he'd have to streak the hallway. (I wondered why he couldn't just put on a robe.)

If you suspect someone is old or infirm, it's also a good idea to tell them the house starts one flight up. It's hard work for some people: I like to park a chair at the landing.

EXPENSES
Keep a tally of what you spend so I can add reimbursement to your check for being here.

Thank you a thousand times! I hope things run smoothly for you. Feel free to call my cell phone if you have any questions at all.

Have fun!

XXOO
Becky